Spiritual Treasures

from
St. Thérèse of Lisieux

A BOOK OF REFLECTIONS AND PRAYERS

D1447349

Spiritual Treasures

from
St. Thérèse *of* Lisieux

A BOOK OF REFLECTIONS AND PRAYERS

EDITED BY CYNTHIA CAVNAR

the WORD
among us®
press

The Word Among Us Press
9639 Doctor Perry Road
Ijamsville, Maryland 21754
www.wordamongus.org
11 10 09 08 07   1 2 3 4 5
ISBN: 978-1-59325-110-9

Cover design by Evelyn Harris
Cover Image Copyright © Office Central de Lisieux
Printed in the United States of America

Library of Congress Cataloging-in-Publication Data
Thérèse, de Lisieux, Saint, 1873-1897.
    [Selections. English. 2007]
    Spiritual treasures from St. Thérèse of Lisieux : a book of reflections
and prayers / edited by Cynthia Cavnar.
        p. cm.
    Originally published: Prayers and meditations of Thérèse of Lisieux.
Ann Arbor, Mich. : Servant Publications, c1992.
    Includes bibliographical references.
    ISBN 978-1-59325-110-9 (alk. paper)
    1. Catholic Church--Prayers and devotions. I. Cavnar, Cindy. II.
Title. III. Title: Spiritual treasures from Saint Thérèse of Lisieux.
    BX2179.T49E5 2007
    242--dc22
                                    2007031690

Contents

LIST OF ABBREVIATIONS

SS Clarke: *Story of a Soul: The Autobiography of St. Thérèse of Lisieux*, translated by John Clarke, OCD (Washington: ICS Publications, 1975)

SS Edmonson: *The Story of a Soul,* translated and edited by Robert J. Edmonson, CJ (Brewster, MA: Paraclete Press, 2006)

GC I and II: *General Correspondence I and II*, translated by John Clarke, OCD (Washington: ICS Publications, 1988)

HLC: *St. Thérèse of Lisieux: Her Last Conversations,* translated by John Clarke, OCD (Washington: ICS Publications, 1977)

MSST: Sr. Geneviève of the Holy Face, *My Sister, Saint Thérèse,* translated by the Carmelite Sisters of New York Conseils et Souvenirs (Rockford, IL: Tan Books, 1997)

STL: *St. Thérèse of Lisieux by Those Who Knew Her,* edited and translated by Christopher O'Mahony, OCD (Huntington, IN: OSV, 1975)

NOTE TO THE READER

The material in the following chapters focuses on key themes in Thérèse's spirituality. It is intended for use in personal prayer and reflection. In each chapter, excerpts from her prayers and meditations follow a major theme and are interspersed with commentary that situates them in her life and spirituality. Each chapter then concludes with a reflection and a prayer.

After reading and reflecting on the prayers and meditations in a particular chapter, you may want to use the closing reflection and prayer to guide you in your own time of personal prayer. Or you may decide to linger over a prayer or meditation earlier in the chapter that seems particularly apt to your situation.

However you use this book, it is my sincere hope that these prayers and meditations will inspire you to love God with all your heart and to seek his will for your life—whatever that involves. Then you will truly be following in the footsteps of Thérèse of Lisieux and in the footsteps of Jesus.

PREFACE

Several years ago, I planned a trip to Rome but ended up in France sort of by mistake. My flight from New York to Rome connected through Paris, but, distracted when booking my ticket, I had failed to arrange the continuing flight for the Rome leg of the trip. I realized my error almost immediately. Having never been to Paris, however, I decided to make the most of it and rearranged my pre-Italy travel to accommodate this new twist. A month later, there I was, on my own for three days in that legendary city.

On the second day, though, it occurred to me that Lisieux was only about 120 miles away, close enough for a quick visit. That afternoon, I caught a train there, hoping that I would arrive before all the places associated with St. Thérèse closed for the day.

The train sped into the countryside, my compartment slowly emptying as other travelers got off at their destinations. Finally, near Lisieux, only one other person remained. She slid down the seat opposite me until we were knee-to-knee.

"You are a pilgrim, too?" the middle-aged French woman said in impeccable English. A pilgrim. I hadn't thought of it that way.

"Well, yes," I said. "I suppose I am."

"And traveling to Lisieux on Thérèse's feast day," she said. "This is excellent."

Oh no, her feast day. How could I have forgotten that October 1 is her feast day? Crowds, long lines at major sites, souvenir vendors hawking bad religious art—I'm not *that* much of a pilgrim.

"Ah," I replied. "Hmmm."

My companion sized up the situation. "The crowds will be gone by the time we arrive," she assured me. "In fact, we are arriving so late that unless you know Lisieux, places will be closed by the time you find your way around. I will take you in hand."

And so she did.

I don't remember this woman's name, but I gleaned that her life had been difficult. Her circumstances remained painful, she said as we pulled into the station, but she had found in St. Thérèse a friend whose prayers and example sustained her. She returned every year to express her gratitude and to visit acquaintances in one of the religious congregations there.

By the time we had walked through the station to the streets of Lisieux, my self-appointed guide had collected two other travelers. She led us all at a trot through back alleys and streets until, turning a corner, there it was before us: the Carmel where Thérèse spent the last nine years of her life.

Our two additional pilgrims went off on their own, but my guide took me inside, pointed out Thérèse's tomb, and said she had something to attend to but would return in fifteen minutes to direct me to Les Buissonnets, Thérèse's family home.

She was true to her word. We soon sped away from the Carmel, cut through a small city garden where Thérèse and her father often walked, and emerged on the main street, where my companion, waving in the direction of Les Buissonnets, told me to turn right a few blocks down. Then, accepting my thanks, she left.

Les Buissonnets was nearly—but not quite—everything I expected. (And aside from the caretaker, I was the only person in the house for the length of my visit.)

I had always been struck by the story of Thérèse's Christmas miracle, as she called it, when she had her "conversion" on the way up the stairs after midnight Mass. In fact, of all the events of Thérèse's life, this was among those that impressed me the most. She was fourteen at the time and a weepy, overly sensitive soul. She had set out her shoes to be filled with presents, as was the custom, but her father found the sight irritating.

Thérèse was on her way upstairs to drop off her hat, when she heard her father express relief that this would be the last year he would have to participate in this childish custom. Rather than dissolve in tears, her typical response to just about anything, she made a conscious choice to get a grip on herself. She joined the family and happily opened her gifts, sweeping her father, who forgot his outburst, into her joy.

This incident—this choice to put aside self-interest for the sake of others—was a turning point in Thérèse's life, helping make all future sacrifices possible.

I had often thought of this miracle-on-the-stairs and envisioned a majestic, curving staircase with lots of gleaming wood and finials. After all, her family was bourgeois. The staircase turned out to be drab and compact, stuck in a corner behind a door; the most you could say for it is that if you wanted to go upstairs or down, it got the job done.

So this is where the great life-changing moment took place, the seemingly insignificant choice that launched Thérèse into the future and, at the outset, neatly captured her Little Way.

Thérèse knew that everyday choices have a cumulative effect, adding up to sanctity or it's opposite. I understood, standing on that staircase, that nearly every moment is ripe with the opportunity to advance in the unaffected holiness and simple goodness that make life better for those around us.

A crucial choice on a nondescript stairwell in a small town in France opened up unsuspected depths of sanctity in one of our greatest saints. Similar unheralded choices are available to each of us every day.

May we choose well, inspired by Thérèse's example and supported by her prayers.

Cynthia Cavnar

INTRODUCTION

Saints, almost by definition, are larger than life—at least in the popular imagination. We want our saints tough, like St. Anthony, who fasted in the desert for eighty-five years. We want them brave, like St. Felicity, who went to her martyrdom only hours after giving birth. We like it if they were notorious sinners prior to their conversion, like St. Camillus, who drank heavily and was addicted to gambling. We're happy if they were exceptionally gentle, like St. Francis of Assisi, or incredibly bright, like St. Augustine. We like saints with a bit of flash, given to visions, workers of miracles.

Judged from this perspective, Thérèse of Lisieux is a major disappointment. She never counseled the pope, fought in the arena, or bantered with the intelligentsia. She had an extremely limited, almost nonexistent experience of phenomena such as visions and ecstasies. Worse yet, she said she wanted to be forgotten, trampled underfoot "like a grain of sand." In fact, she led a very sheltered life in the cultural confines of nineteenth-century bourgeois France. In just about every category, Thérèse comes up short.

Or maybe she doesn't. Perhaps the problem lies not with Thérèse or the other saints but with our expectations of them. We are an achievement-oriented society focused on wealth, power, and accomplishment. Whether we intend to or not, many of us apply this same standard to the saints. It's not enough for them to be holy; they also have to found great missionary orders, convert enormous numbers of people, have visions, and die as martyrs.

It may be that we're more comfortable with the external and less sure of the internal. Nevertheless, there is no other standard with which to measure the saints than their inner life with God. Nothing matters less, when assessing the saints, than what they accomplished. Nothing matters more than the answer to the question, Did they do the will of God?

This is particularly true when considering Thérèse of Lisieux. Obviously, a woman who spent the last nine years of her life in a cloistered convent and died at the age of twenty-four didn't achieve much in worldly terms. She conquered herself, and she attained union with God, and that's about it. By the only standard that counts—the gospel—she was a phenomenal success.

The Cross behind the Flower

In spite of her low profile during her life, Thérèse is a popular saint today. In fact, she even enjoyed a measure of popularity among Christians in the years immediately following her death. This was partially due to her startling deathbed promise to spend her heaven doing good on earth. She was true to her word, and as astonishing accounts of her intercession began to circulate, her fame spread.

Many people, too, found her Little Way of holiness, based on small sacrifices and acts of kindness, helpful in living the Christian life.

To a certain extent, however, Thérèse's popularity is based on a false reading of her life and personality. In the reverse of the typical situation, where we admire a saint for his or her accomplishments, Thérèse is admired for what is perceived as a childlike docility. No need to worry that Thérèse will nag about the poor or challenge authority or ask hard questions. She was sweet, submissive, and a saint, to boot. Those who like their saints non-threatening find this version of Thérèse satisfying.

Thérèse can indeed appear passive to those who give her a shallow reading or who encounter some of the sentimental material written about her. Her nickname, "the Little Flower," doesn't help. It may have been charming in nineteenth-century France, but today it conjures up images of a delicate helplessness at odds with our hard-edged culture. Even Thérèse's sister Céline had her doubts about the name. She was afraid that too many people failed to see the cross behind the Little Flower.

Thérèse is partially responsible for the misunderstanding. What are we to make of a saint who calls herself the little toy of the baby Jesus? More often than we'd like, she slips into this naive, excessively sweet prose. The reader occasionally needs considerable determination to plow through her letters and her autobiography, *Story of a Soul*.

Actually Thérèse's writing style is nothing more than a reflection of her own youth and of the French middle-class culture in which she grew up. It may also be due, in some part, to changes that her sister Pauline made to the manuscript before it was published. Nevertheless, it has earned her an unenviable and undeserved reputation as a lightweight.

Thomas Merton, the Trappist monk and author, said he was surprised, when he first became acquainted with Thérèse, to discover that she "was . . . not just a mute pious little doll in the imaginations of a lot of sentimental old women. . . . No sooner had I got a faint glimpse of the real character and the real spirituality of St. Thérèse, than I was immediately and strongly attracted to her." "Not only was she a saint," he concluded, "but a great saint, one of the greatest: tremendous!"[1]

Thomas Merton was a cautious man with a probing intellect, never guilty of sentimentalism—typical, in fact, of many today who are likely to dismiss Thérèse. Merton took a hard look, however, and liked what he saw. Undoubtedly, there is more to the Little Flower than either her name or her girlish reputation would imply.

The Fruit of Devout Parents

Thérèse Martin was born on January 2, 1873, in Alençon, France, the last of nine children. Much has been written about her remarkable parents, Louis and Zélie Guérin Martin, and they are under consideration for canonization themselves. Five of their children survived, all of them girls, and all of whom entered the convent.

Louis and Zélie, too, had originally hoped to enter the religious life. Louis set his sights on the Augustinian canons of the Great St. Bernard Hospice in the Alps. Together with their famous dogs, these monks rescued travelers who were lost in the snow or stranded on mountain passes. Their quiet way of life, coupled with occasional feats of derring-do, appealed to the young Martin.

Louis visited the hospice, but the prior told him to apply when he had learned Latin, necessary to a monastic career. He returned to his hometown of Alençon and studied intensely for a year. Then, for unknown reasons, he gave up. It may be that he was unable to master Latin, or he may have suffered from poor health, or he may simply have misjudged his vocation. At any rate, Louis turned to a career in watch making and repair. He opened a shop in Alençon in 1850.

About this same time, Zélie Guérin, also a native of Alençon, learned that she, too, had no future in the religious life. Zélie was rejected by the order to which she applied, the Sisters of St. Vincent de Paul. The mother superior gave no reason other than to say that Zélie didn't have a vocation.

This unexpected turn of events left Zélie adrift. She went to the Blessed Mother in prayer. One day she heard an interior voice very clearly say, "Go and make Point d'Alençon," the handmade lace for which Alençon was famous. Zélie learned the art and established herself in business. Within a few years, she became enormously successful.

Louis and Zélie might have continued on their separate paths for years, successful, unmarried, and pious, but for a combination of circumstances. Louis' mother was eager for him to marry and, having met Zélie, decided that she was the woman for him.

For her part, Zélie one day happened to pass by a tall, serious man whose appearance struck her. Again, an interior voice spoke, telling her that this was the man she was going to marry. It turned out to be Louis Martin. At this point, Louis' mother intervened, and the two of them were soon married.

After this happy resolution, we would expect the Martins to begin producing children. However, their story took an unusual turn. Louis and Zélie, in imitation of the Blessed Virgin and St. Joseph, decided to have a celibate marriage. Actually, the decision was probably more Louis' than Zélie's. She had prayed, on being rejected by the convent, that God would let her marry and bear many children. These would be consecrated to him.

Ten months after the wedding, a priest convinced the Martins to reverse their decision. Children followed in quick succession, to the parents' great delight. "I am madly in love with children," Zélie said from her lively home. "I was born to have them" (GC II 1199).

By the time Thérèse arrived on the scene, the family had taken its final form. Marie was almost thirteen years old; Pauline was ten; Léonie, nine; and Céline, four. The Martins had endured the deaths of two infant sons, an infant daughter, and five-year-old Hélène, whom Zélie referred to as "a lovely jewel."

Pious but Real

For awhile, it looked as if Thérèse might soon follow her siblings into eternity. She rallied, though, and developed into a healthy, sturdy little girl. The high religious standards of the home and the deep affection of Louis and Zélie set the stage for the type of devout childhood we have come to expect of the saints. Thérèse doesn't let us down.

The writer Flannery O'Connor said that "stories of pious children tend to be false. . . . I have never cared to read about little boys who build altars and play they are priests, or about little girls who dress up as nuns, or about those pious Protestant children who lack this equipment but brighten the corners where they are."[2]

In Thérèse's case, O'Connor was wrong about the stories' being false. They are abundant and were confirmed by many witnesses during the canonization process. O'Connor may have been right when she implied that a stream of such stories tends to be tedious if not unbelievable.

Thérèse was as good as children get, with a clear view of heaven and a great love of God. Still, she had spirit. Her mother described her as bright, mischievous, and completely stubborn. She had something of a temper, occasionally rolled around on the floor when she didn't get her way, and once stamped her foot at the maid and called her a brat. One has to look long and hard to find similar incidents.

Thérèse expressed herself in unusual ways. In a letter, her mother recounted a conversation she had with Thérèse when the child was three. "Oh! How I wish you were dead, dear little mother," Thérèse said. When Zélie scolded her, Thérèse assured her mother that she had said it only "'so that you many go to heaven, since you say we must die to go there.'" Zélie added that Thérèse "wishes also death of her father when she is in her transports of love" (GC II 1218–19).

Unfortunately, Thérèse's hopes for her mother were realized much too soon. When Thérèse was four years old, Zélie Martin died of breast cancer. This marked the beginning of what Thérèse called the saddest period of her life, which lasted for ten years. She lost her happy disposition and became wary and oversensitive, crying at the least provocation. It wasn't until Thérèse was fourteen that she achieved the great interior victory that liberated her from hypersensitivity and launched her on the path to spiritual freedom.

A Father's Motherly Love

Psychology places great emphasis on the role of the father in forming a child's notion of God. An affectionate, supportive father is more likely to produce a secure child, able to experience God's love. In the aftermath of Zélie's death, Louis Martin fulfilled his role beyond any child's expectations.

Thérèse felt that her father's love was enriched by a strong motherly love, she wrote in her autobiography. Louis and Thérèse often went fishing together, and he took her on walks, picnics, daily visits to the Blessed Sacrament, and little vacations to the sea or to visit friends. He called her his "little queen," and though he was deeply devoted to her, managed to avoid spoiling her.

Thérèse speaks of him frequently. "I cannot say how much I loved Papa," she wrote. "Everything in him caused me to admire him" (SS Clarke 48). After her work was done, she used to play by his side in the garden. She had the most fun, she said, soaking seeds and bark in water and then giving her father this "tea" in a pretty teacup. He'd smile, accept her offering, and pretend to sip.

He gave her a patch of garden, where she grew flowers and decorated little altars in a niche in the wall. Decorating done, she'd drag her father over, and he would please her by launching into fervent praise, convincing her that she had produced a masterpiece. "How could I possibly express the tenderness which Papa showered upon his queen? There are things the heart feels but which the tongue and even the mind cannot express" (SS Clarke 37).

The picture Thérèse paints is ideal and, according to her sisters, accurate. They were not jealous of her, they explained at the canonization proceedings, because their father was warm and affectionate with all of them. True, his love for his youngest daughter was unique, but they could see that Thérèse brought him great comfort.

The bond Louis forged with Thérèse was vital to her spiritual development. She was an incredibly secure individual with high self-esteem and remarkable confidence in God. Interestingly, however, this warm relationship did not spare Thérèse the tremendous aridity she experienced as a nun in her relationship with God.

Psychologically speaking, the strong love of her earthly father should have led Thérèse, as an adult, into a warm, lively relationship with her heavenly Father. Although there was plenty of warmth on Thérèse's side, however, she generally met silence and even, toward the end, what felt like indifference from the other side.

Throughout her religious life, Thérèse had virtually no consolation in prayer or experience of God's presence. She felt nothing of an emotional nature to draw her forward in her vocation. During the last year and a half of her life, she lost her belief in heaven and struggled with despair and doubt.

In short, in spite of a childhood soaked in love, Thérèse still had to make a leap of faith: God asked her to believe in him even though she didn't experience him. Thérèse's warm relationship with her father prepared her to make an intellectual assent to faith even in the absence of feelings. It did not give her the sort of cozy experience of God we might have expected.

Crybaby No More

While Thérèse was basking in her father's love, her sisters, especially Pauline, were lavishing her with motherly love. Upon Zélie's death, Thérèse asked Pauline to be her mother, and Céline, who was eight years old at the time, asked Marie to be hers. Both Pauline and Marie outdid themselves in their care for their little sisters. Even in her autobiography, Thérèse addresses Pauline as her "little mother."

Zélie's brother, Isidore Guérin, and his wife, Céline, helped the Martin family cope. Soon after the funeral, the Martins moved to Les Buissonnets, a house in Lisieux near their cousins. An extremely happy relationship sprang up between these two pious families. One of the Guérin daughters, Marie, later joined the Martin girls in the Carmel at Lisieux.

Once again, however, Thérèse's world came crashing down: Pauline entered the Carmelite convent when Thérèse was almost ten years old. She later said that the blow was so great that she felt as if Jesus had snatched her mother away. The agony she experienced seemed to open her eyes to life as it really was—a daily reality marked, she said, by suffering and repeated separations.

A few months later, in what may have been in part a psychological reaction to Pauline's departure, Thérèse suffered a complete collapse and hovered near death. Her father, in despair, arranged for a series of Masses to be said for her recovery at the shrine of Our Lady of Victories in Paris.

The family was devoted to Mary, and a statue of Our Lady of Victories stood near Thérèse's bed. During the course of the novena, Thérèse took a turn for the worse. One day, however, when Thérèse looked at the statue, she saw Mary smile at her. Instantly, Thérèse recovered her health.

Unfortunately, the miraculous intervention caused a sensation. Wanting to hear the details, people badgered Thérèse for information. The persistent questioning robbed her of her joy in the event, and she endured such humiliation over the experience that she could only regard herself with contempt. She wouldn't be able to express the depth of her suffering except in heaven, she wrote.

All in all, Thérèse seems to have been a rather gloomy child during this period of her life. She attended school, where she excelled academically but had trouble making friends. It's not difficult to see why; she admits that she wasn't very cheerful, nor was she adept at playing games. "Often during the recreations, I leaned against a tree, . . . giving myself up to serious reflections! I had invented a game which pleased me, and it was to bury the poor little birds we found dead under the trees. Many of the students wanted to help me, and so our cemetery became very beautiful" (SS Clarke 81).

Later, Thérèse spoke of her difficulty making friends as a blessing. She had an ardent nature and an intense longing to be loved, which she felt could have created problems. "I have no merit at all . . . in not giving myself up to the love of creatures. I was preserved from it only through God's mercy," she reflected. "I know that without him, I could have fallen as low as St. Mary Magdalene" (SS Clarke 83). She was grateful, she said, that she had no real knack for making herself attractive to others.

Thérèse may not have been the life of the party, but she was making remarkable spiritual progress. This was due to her own nature but also to the intense spirituality of her home. Marie, who prepared her for first Communion , was quite eloquent, and it seemed to Thérèse that Marie's ardent spirit became her own. "Just as famous warriors taught their children the art of war, so Marie spoke to me about life's struggles and of the palm given to the victors" (SS Clarke 74).

On the other hand, Marie was sensible. Thérèse told her that she wanted to practice mental prayer, but Marie said no—Thérèse was already devout enough. Thérèse had the last word, however. She used to go into a space behind her bed, shut off by a curtain. There she sat and thought about God, life, and eternity. Later, she realized that she had in fact been practicing contemplative prayer even though she didn't know it. God taught her in secret, she wrote in her autobiography.

The pace of Thérèse's spiritual development quickened with the reception of her first Communion, when she was eleven. On that occasion, she achieved a mystical union with God, the type of experience that would soon be little more than a memory. She may have had a glimpse of the spiritual dryness that awaited her when she received Communion again not too long after.

On that occasion, she said, "I felt born within my heart a great desire to suffer. . . . Up until that time, I had suffered without loving suffering, but since this day I felt a real love for it" (SS Clarke 79). It was not because she loved pain. Rather, she knew the redemptive value of suffering as demonstrated by Jesus on the cross.

Thérèse regarded this moment as one of the greatest graces of her life. Shortly after, she received the Sacrament of Confirmation and, with it, the ability to suffer. She felt that she was embarking on the martyrdom that would be her life.

First, however, Thérèse had to overcome her tendency to be a crybaby, as she frankly called herself. She had fought against this hypersensitivity for ten years, with little success.

She knew that her touchiness made it hard for people to be around her. Instead of apologizing and moving on when she offended someone, she cried. When she finally began to pull herself together, she would break down and cry again over having cried in the first place. Nothing she did, nor anything anyone said, helped her overcome this extreme sensitivity. Her family, fed up with this behavior, told her that she cried so much as a child, she'd have no tears left to shed as an adult.

Her liberation was the "complete conversion" that occurred after midnight Mass on Christmas Day 1886. On her way up the stairs at Les Buissonnets, Thérèse overheard her father express his annoyance that she had set her shoes by the fireplace, expecting to find presents in them.

She hesitated, on the verge of tears. Céline urged her not to go back down, certain that she would end up crying. But something was different, and Thérèse knew it. In an instant, she later said, Jesus had changed her heart. She forced back her tears, entered the living room as though nothing had happened, and joyfully opened her gifts. At that moment, she claimed, she regained the strength of soul she had lost when her mother died. She also recovered her happy disposition to such a degree that later, in the convent, she was known for her wit and sense of humor.

This was the start of the third period of her life, Thérèse wrote, "the most beautiful and the most filled with graces from heaven. The work I had been unable to do in ten years was done by Jesus in one instant, contenting himself with my good will which was never lacking" (SS Clarke 98).

Thérèse received another significant grace at the same moment. "[God] made me a fisher of souls," she declared. "I experienced a great desire to work for the conversion of sinners, a desire I hadn't felt so intensely before. . . . The cry of Jesus on the cross sounded continually in my heart: 'I thirst.'" She wanted to quench this thirst by presenting him with repentant sinners. "I felt myself consumed with a thirst for souls," Thérèse said (SS Clarke 99).

As a sort of test of this new direction, she prayed for the conversion of an unrepentant murderer named Pranzini. The condemned man remained obdurate. Moments before his execution, however, he seized a crucifix offered him by a priest and kissed it three times. This was a startling response from a merciful God, Thérèse felt, and it fired her with an overwhelming desire to win souls for him.

With Courage and Persistence

Thérèse claimed that she wanted to be a nun from the age of three. Now that she was fourteen, she was convinced that her time had come. Marie had joined Pauline in the Lisieux Carmel, and Léonie had made a brief, unsuccessful attempt to enter the Poor Clares.

Louis had willingly surrendered these daughters to the religious life, but it had been difficult. It would be even more so with Thérèse, his favorite. Nevertheless, she summoned up her courage, and on the feast of Pentecost 1887 she approached her father for the necessary permission.

Perhaps this moment more than any validates Thérèse's immense regard for her father. She came upon him as he sat in the garden in the early evening sunlight, utterly at peace. There were tears in her eyes, and he held her close and asked what was troubling his "little queen." Perhaps Louis sensed what was to come, for he got up as if he wanted to conceal his own feelings. He began to walk slowly up and down, holding her close to him. They both wept as she pleaded her case, but he was convinced of her vocation and made no attempt to discourage her. God honored him greatly, he said with feeling, by asking him to surrender his children.

Now that she had her father's permission, Thérèse thought no obstacles remained to thwart her entry into Carmel. She failed to take into account her age. The nuns themselves were ready to accept her, but that was not enough. First she had to persuade everyone from her Uncle Isidore to the bishop that she was indeed mature enough for the sacrifice.

Louis helped her apply to the proper authorities for permission to join the order and then took Thérèse and Céline on a pilgrimage to Rome. If they couldn't resolve the problem before their departure, he said, he intended to have Thérèse speak to the pope himself. And so she did.

The great moment came on November 20, 1887. The members of the Martins' tour group crowded into the audience hall, each awaiting his turn to approach

Pope Leo XIII to receive his blessing. They were absolutely forbidden to speak, a priest warned them, but Thérèse boldly stuck to her plan. She knelt before the pope, once again in tears. "Most Holy Father," she blurted, "I have a great favor to ask you. . . . In honor of your jubilee, permit me to enter Carmel at the age of fifteen."

A hubbub broke out. One of the priests, irritated, told the pope that the matter was in the hands of the authorities. "Well, my child," Pope Leo said to Thérèse, "do what the superiors tell you!" Thérèse had come a long way for this moment, and she was not about to be put off. She clasped her hands, placed them on the pope's knees, and made a final effort. "Oh! Holy Father," she pleaded. "If you say yes, everybody will agree!" "Go, go," he responded, "you will enter if God wills it" (SS Clarke 134–35). The determined Thérèse was about to speak again, when two guards and a priest physically removed her.

Thérèse was in despair over what she perceived as her failed mission, but others were impressed by her courage and persistence. There was still some opposition to her request, but she eventually prevailed. On April 9, 1888, Thérèse entered the Lisieux Carmel at the age of fifteen.

In the Convent

Religious life was exactly as Thérèse expected. The prayers, the deprivations, the food, the chores, the nuns themselves—nothing surprised her. She made a smooth transition, but her vocation was immediately put to the test.

The prioress of the convent, Mother Marie de Gonzague, was a capable, efficient administrator, but she had a difficult personality. She easily flew into a temper, criticized the other nuns, was jealous, self-important, and had no sympathy for the elderly, sick, or weak. Thérèse soon discovered that there were significant problems in the Carmel, many of which could be traced to the prioress.

Mother Marie had encouraged and welcomed Thérèse's entry, but to all appearances her enthusiasm waned once Thérèse was present. She was harsh and demanding, and in her infrequent conferences with the young postulant, Mother Marie spent most of the time berating her. "I was unable to meet her without having to kiss the floor," Thérèse recalled. "Once, I remember having left a cobweb in the cloister; she said to me before the whole community: 'We can easily see that our cloisters are swept by a child of fifteen! Go and take that cobweb away and be more careful in the future. . . .' She acted this way in every-thing concerning me" (SS Clarke 150).

Appearances to the contrary, the prioress was im-pressed with Thérèse. She never would have expected such sound judgment in someone of fifteen, she later said. She felt that an individual of Thérèse's excep-tional maturity and holiness should not be coddled. Thérèse accepted the ill treatment out of obedience, but also because she genuinely loved Mother Marie and felt that the prioress's method was the right one.

Thérèse's greatest source of suffering at this time was not Mother Marie but the rapid physical and mental decline of her father, who had suffered a small stroke prior to the pilgrimage to Rome. After Thérèse's entry into Carmel, he endured a series of strokes that left him increasingly incapacitated. One day, he disappeared only to turn up a few days later at the harbor in Le Havre. The family placed him in a mental institution where, in his lucid moments, he was well aware of his fate.

It was the most distressing trial a man could face, he said, but his daughters drew comfort from the fact that he both accepted his condition and offered it up as a prayer. He told a doctor that he needed a hu-miliation since he had never experienced one. Used to commanding, he humbly acknowledged that now he must obey.

He paid a last visit to Carmel shortly before he died, his helpless body tucked into a wheelchair. It was a sad meeting, according to Thérèse. "When he was leaving and we were saying goodbye, he lifted his eyes to heaven and remained that way a long time and had only one word with which to express his thoughts: 'In heaven!'" meaning they would meet again in heaven (SS Clarke 176). He died in 1894.

Simply Love

All the elements of Thérèse's spirituality were in place when she entered the convent, needing only fuller development. Her approach was refreshingly straightforward and uncomplicated. A perceptive older nun once told Thérèse that her soul was very simple. She'd become more simple yet, the nun said, as she progressed in perfection. "The closer one approaches to God, the simpler one becomes" (SS Clarke 151).

Still, Thérèse's path to sanctity sometimes looks more simple than it really is. Often, it is reduced to nothing more than her Little Way, with its small, daily acts of thoughtfulness and sacrifice. Thérèse, however, would have abandoned the Little Way in an instant if she had thought it was the sum of the spiritual life. What really mattered to Thérèse was God himself. The Little Way was simply the approach she used to love him and her neighbor.

It's difficult to do justice to Thérèse's intense, exclusive love for the Lord. Her sister Pauline observed that just as the rest of us breathe air, so Thérèse breathed the love of God. Thérèse couldn't imagine what more she could enjoy after her death than she already enjoyed. She acknowledged that, yes, she would see God, but she was already completely in his company here on earth. She didn't always experience him, we know, but she was with him in the sense that she was totally given over to him.

Thérèse had an electrifying awareness of the importance of God's love for us and our love for him, particularly in the person of Jesus. She wanted no one but Jesus, she declared, and she asked him to preserve her devotion so that she never sought anyone but him, that he would always and forever be everything to her. She was overcome when she considered the enormity of his sacrifice on the cross: he had pushed his love to the extreme, and she was determined to respond in kind.

Thérèse concluded that her vocation was nothing less than love itself. She wanted to be everything for God, from apostle to martyr, but realized that was impossible. "My vocation is love," she decided. "I understood that love comprised all vocations, that love was everything, that it embraced all times and places . . . in a word, that it was eternal!" (SS Clarke 194).

Thérèse put a different spin on this conclusion than we might expect. Her vocation included receiving God's love and giving it to others, which seems conventional enough. But she had a keen sense that God himself longs for our love. Many people either refuse to give it to him or don't realize how intensely he wants it. God doesn't need that love, she knew, but nevertheless, he yearns for it.

With that in mind, in 1895 Thérèse offered herself as a "victim" to this love. She knew that some people offered themselves to God as victims of his justice, to draw his punishment away from sinners onto themselves. She wanted to draw down his mercy. "O my God! Will your justice alone find souls willing to immolate themselves as victims? Does not your merciful love need them too? On every side this love is unknown, rejected" (SS Clarke 180).

After she made this consecration of herself, she said, her life became a continuous offering of perfect love—she was immersed in and flooded with love.

But not an experiential love. The great mystery of Thérèse's life, of course, is the utter silence God adopted after she entered the convent. She who had enjoyed his warmth and compassion now found herself abruptly cut off.

During her retreat before her profession, for example, she felt nearly abandoned by God and utterly without consolation. In her thanksgivings after receiving Communion, she felt his presence less than ever. In a note to her sister Marie, Thérèse wrote that the Lord never made himself known to her, nor could she hear his voice within; she decided that her consolation in this life would be not to have any consolation.

Thérèse's response to this unexpected turn of events was nothing short of heroic. "Jesus does not will that we love him for his gifts," she insisted. "It is he himself who must be our reward" (GC II 809). She hadn't come to the convent to experience God or to feel good; she was there solely to love him and to win souls for him through her sacrifices. She explicitly surrendered any desire to receive a love that she could feel, and she said, instead, that her whole desire was to give Jesus a love that *he* would feel and to bring others to that same intense, disinterested love for him.

Thérèse's sufferings were not confined to her prayer life. The Little Way, so often misinterpreted as the mere performance of ones duties, was a daily exercise in martyrdom for Thérèse. Zélie had claimed that her daughter was unconquerably stubborn. Thérèse retained that iron will throughout her life and bent it toward the service of others only at extreme cost to herself.

But bend it she did, countless times a day. Her sister Céline, who entered Carmel after Louis' death, provided an example. Thérèse used to hang around the other nuns after her work was done, Céline recalled. She wanted the sisters to feel free to ask for her help, which they invariably did. Céline then gave an amusing insight into her own attitude when she added that she often tried to show Thérèse how she could avoid this service. Needless to say, Céline's tips were in vain. Thérèse's strategy, of course, was deliberate: she wanted to sacrifice herself for one and all, according to their needs.

Thérèse wasn't "naturally" disposed to lay down her life. She was able to do so only because she trained herself to do so day in and day out. She took advantage of even the smallest opportunities to die to herself—this is why her way is little—and found there sufficient material to achieve sanctity. This daily crucifixion gives the lie to those who perceive Thérèse as insipid.

Thérèse wasn't naturally inclined toward humility, either, although it is a cornerstone of her Little Way. She took the virtue far beyond the common understanding of humility as a modest opinion of oneself. She even went beyond the notion of being despised, insulted, or mocked. Thérèse wanted to be forgotten. Why? For the glory of Jesus, she said. Any attention that came to her would only detract from the glory due to him.

Like St. Paul, Thérèse actually took delight in her imperfections. "My power is made perfect in weakness," the Lord said to Paul. Paul replied, "I will all the more gladly boast of my weaknesses, that the power of Christ may rest upon me" (2 Corinthians 12:9). If the other nuns discovered her faults, so what? In fact, what a blessing! This was an opportunity to practice humility, Thérèse said, for true humility involves not only a realistic appraisal of your faults but also genuine joy in discovering that others see your faults and share your opinion.

Pain for the Conversion of Sinners

Thérèse was certainly more than "a pious little doll," more than the demure child of overwrought imaginations. She had the advantage of a secure childhood, but that didn't spare her the total interior stripping she endured as a nun. A barren prayer life? Ill-tempered nuns? Insufficient food? An unbalanced mother superior? Thérèse waded into the fray with gusto and displayed a measure of self-control and charity that was nothing short of astonishing.

Perhaps nothing brings her closer to the soul of the twenty-first century, however, than the last year and a half of her life. As if anticipating the doubts that would plague future generations, Thérèse experienced an almost complete loss of faith. She struggled with outright disbelief until the moment of her death.

This "dark night of the soul" came upon her unexpectedly. During Lent of 1896, she had twice vomited blood, a harbinger of the tuberculosis that would eventually kill her. She was delighted at the thought of her approaching death, she said, because her faith was clear and firmly grounded. Not for long.

"Jesus . . . permitted my soul to be invaded by the thickest darkness, and that the thought of heaven, up until then so sweet to me, be no longer anything but the cause of struggle and torment." Her soul was smothered, she said, and she couldn't even imagine a place like heaven.

In one of the most poignant passages of her autobiography, Thérèse wrote that the voice of unbelievers mocked her from the darkness. "Advance," the voices jeered, "Rejoice in death which will give you not what you hope for but a night still more profound, the night of nothingness!" (SS Clarke 211, 213).

At the same time, Thérèse began a long, agonizing physical decline that led to unimaginable suffering. On one occasion, she cried out that she never would have thought it possible to suffer so much. The last few months were a nightmare of pain, unrelieved by sedatives. Mother Marie, true to form, thought a Carmelite ought to be able to handle a bit of suffering.

Thérèse could. This was in part because she longed to be a martyr, but primarily because she wanted to offer her pain for the conversion of sinners. This thirst for souls was the only explanation she could give for her suffering. Thérèse endured it all with her customary serenity and joy, leading the doctor to pronounce her "an angel."

Still, her suffering was unrelentingly difficult, and she found her trial of faith incomprehensible. Nor did she have the consolation of sharing her thoughts.

She kept them to herself, Celine reported after Therese's death, for fear of influencing others or even blaspheming.

Thérèse triumphed, in a staggering display of self-control and complete submission to the will of God. Stripped of all solace, she realized that in the end she simply had to trust in God. "Suffering can attain extreme limits, but I'm sure God will never abandon me" (HLC 73). She didn't regret those words even as her final slide toward death began. On September 29, the day before she died, she cried out that she couldn't take it any more and asked for prayer. Shortly after, however, she pulled herself together and said to God that yes, she wanted it all.

Her last agony began on the afternoon of September 30. Her sister Pauline recounted that Thérèse's features were distorted, her hands had turned purple, her feet were like ice, and she shook all over. Sweat poured down her face, and she cried out involuntarily as she struggled to breathe. She gasped that the chalice was full to overflowing, that she was suffering but seemed unable to die. She had prayed so hard, she said, but found no relief.

The nuns had been gathered around her bed in prayer, but Mother Marie sent them away when it seemed that Thérèse was holding her own. Thérèse, dismayed, asked if this was not indeed her final agony, the moment of her death. Mother Marie said that it might be a few more hours. "All right, then, let's go on," Thérèse bravely responded. "I wouldn't want the time of suffering cut short. Oh, I love him. My God, I love you" (STL 69).

With that, Thérèse fell back gently, and Mother Marie hastily reassembled the nuns. Thérèse's face was transformed by a look of great joy. Suddenly, she sat up and opened her eyes. She gazed unblinkingly on the area just above the statue of Our Lady that stood by her bed. She stayed that way for a minute or two, her face serene and filled with happiness. Then she closed her eyes and died.

A Saint for Modern Times

Many nuns live holy lives, die holy deaths, and are forgotten. Thérèse knew that her name would endure. Her autobiography would do much good, she said, and she warned her sisters to publish it promptly after her death. If there was any delay, she warned, Satan would work to ensure that it was never published.

The essays that were to become her autobiography had not initially been written for publication, though.

During a term as prioress, Pauline had asked Thérèse to write down her memories of her childhood, as a sort of keepsake for the family. Later, at Pauline's urging, Mother Marie ordered Thérèse to continue the story, which she completed three months before her death.

Story of a Soul was published a year later, and Thérèse's words proved prophetic. The book swept the world. Within a few years, reports of miracles attributed to her intercession began to flood Rome. A clamor arose for her canonization, and the process was completed in twenty-eight years—an extraordinarily speedy accomplishment.

Thérèse has been remembered, too, because she seems determined not to be forgotten—not for her own sake, but for ours. "If God answers my desires," she said, "my heaven will be spent on earth until the end of the world. Yes, I want to spend my heaven in doing good on earth" (HLC 102). She promised that she would let fall "a shower of roses," answers to prayer.

Thérèse has been as good as her word, which comes as no surprise. The church, in fact, teaches that there is an ongoing relationship between those who have died and the faithful on earth. This communion of saints means that our responsibility to one another doesn't end with death. The saints in heaven intercede for the faithful on earth; the faithful on earth pray for the souls in purgatory. We're all in it for the long haul.

Thérèse has made her intentions abundantly clear in this regard. A sheltered nun who died young may seem an odd saint for modern times. But Thérèse accomplished two feats that elude many in our over-stimulated culture: she conquered herself, and she developed a clear understanding of the nature of love. She's ready to help others do the same, a point that Pope John Paul II underscored by naming her a doctor of the church in 1997.

"Don't worry about impressive achievements," Thérèse would say, if we could talk to her today. "They don't amount to much. Love God. Serve your neighbor. Avoid sin. Stay humble."

And ask Thérèse to help. She won't disappoint.

1. Thomas Merton, *Seven Story Mountain*, (New York: Harcourt Brace Jovanovich, 1976), 353–54.

2. Flannery O'Connor, *Mystery and Manners*, Sally and Robert Fitzgerald, ed. (New York: Farrar, Strauss & Giroux, 1969), 213.

Chapter One

To Love Him and to Be Loved by Him

One day when Thérèse was three or four years old, she and her sister Céline were playing together. Their older sister, Léonie, having decided that she was too old for dolls, brought a basketful of her doll clothing and accessories to the younger girls. She told them to take what they wanted. Céline modestly took a little bundle of silk braid, but Thérèse, declaring she wanted it all, took the entire basket.

The incident is vintage Thérèse. She was an all-or-nothing sort of individual. When she wanted something, whether doll clothes as a child or humility as an adult, she went after it full tilt.

Most of all, Thérèse wanted the love of God. This was everything to her, the key to her spirituality and the core of her existence. To love him and to be loved by him made all other sacrifices possible.

Like many saints, Thérèse speaks with passion and intensity about the love of God. Referring to Jesus, she said that she wanted to love him better than he had ever been loved. He was her only friend, she wrote, her first friend, the only one she loved, the only one who was everything to her.

Nothing could keep her from him—not sin, not fear of his justice, not discouragement, not personal weakness. She urged people to throw their sins into the all-consuming furnace of God's love. When they do so with childlike confidence, she said, there can be no doubt that their faults will be entirely consumed.

If we repent for sin, that act of love repairs everything, Thérèse asserted. Not only does Jesus forget our failings and refuse to recall them, but he opens himself wholeheartedly to us.

Thérèse's confidence in God allowed her to speak to him with a striking but utterly childlike boldness—with a limitless audacity, her sister Pauline said. Thérèse had no uncertainty about God's unquenchable love for his creatures. Her way was not that of fear, she said, but was instead full of confidence and love.

Even in the face of incredible suffering, she maintained her conviction. Her last words, uttered when she was in so much pain that she could barely speak, were, "Oh, I love him. . . . My God, I love you."

Suffering, Love, and Abandonment

Thérèse wanted to suffer both to prove her love for God and to do penance for the souls of sinners.

As she matured, however, she focused less on suffering and more on abandonment to the will of God.

I no longer have any desire, unless it is to love Jesus passionately. My childish desires have all flown away. . . .

I don't desire suffering or death, either, and yet I love both of them. But it is love alone that draws me. For a long time I desired them both. I possessed suffering, and I thought I was touching the shores of heaven. Now it's abandonment alone that guides me—I have no other compass!

I can ask for nothing fervently any more except the perfect accomplishment of God's will in my soul [Matthew 6:10], without created things being able to place any obstacle in its path. I can say these words from the spiritual canticle of our father St. John of the Cross: "In the interior cell of my Beloved, I drank, and when I went out, in all that plain I no longer was familiar with anything, and I lost the flock that I had previously been following. My soul was fully engaged with all its resources at its service. I no longer keep watch over a flock, I no longer have any other office, because now my entire practice is to Love!" (SS Edmonson 201–2)

We have only the short moments of our life to love Jesus, and the devil knows this well, and so he tries to consume our life in useless works. (GC I 568–69)

Ever since I have been given the grace to understand also the love of the heart of Jesus, I admit that it has expelled all fear from my heart. The remembrance of my faults humbles me, draws me never to depend on my strength which is only weakness, but this remembrance speaks to me of mercy and love even more.

When we cast our faults with entire filial confidence into the devouring fire of love, how would these not be consumed beyond return?

I know there are some saints who spent their life in the practice of astonishing mortifications to expiate their sins, but what of it: "There are many mansions in the house of my heavenly Father" [John 14:2], Jesus has said, and it is because of this that I follow the way he is tracing out for me. I try to be no longer occupied with myself in anything, and I abandon myself to what Jesus sees fit to do in my soul, for I have not chosen an austere life to expiate my faults but those of others. (GC II 1133–34)

Jesus is a hidden treasure, an inestimable good which few souls can find, for it is hidden, and the world loves what sparkles. Ah! If Jesus had willed to show himself to all souls with his ineffable gifts, no doubt there is not one of them that would have despised him. However, he does not will that we love him for his gifts, he himself must be our reward. (GC II 808–9)

Even when I might have on my conscience all the sins that can be committed, I would go with a heart broken with repentance to throw myself into Jesus' arms, because I know how much he cherishes the prodigal who comes back to him [Luke 15:20-24]. It's not because God, in his kind mercy, has preserved my soul from mortal sin that I rise and go to him in confidence and love. (SS Edmonson 297)

You know, God, I've never desired anything else than to love you. My ambition is for no other glory. Your love informed me beginning in my childhood. It grew with me, and now it's a chasm the depths of which I cannot fathom. Love attracts love, so, my Jesus, mine shoots up toward you. It would like to fill up the chasm that draws it, but alas! It's not even a drop of dew lost in the ocean!

To love you as you love me, I have to borrow your own love; only then do I find rest. Oh my Jesus, it's perhaps an illusion, but it seems to me that you can't fill a soul with more love than you've filled mine. It's because of that, that I dare to ask you to love those whom you have given me as you have loved me. One day, in heaven, if I discover that you love them more than me, I'll rejoice at that, since I recognize even now that those souls merit your love much more than I do. But here below I cannot conceive of a greater immensity of love than the one that it has pleased you to pour out so lavishly on me, without any merit on my part. (SS Edmonson 293)

A Victim of God's Love

Thérèse had heard of people who offered themselves to God as "victims" of his justice, in order to turn away his punishment from sinners, taking that punishment on themselves. She admitted that she was not attracted to this. Instead, Thérèse decided to offer herself as a victim of God's love in order to draw that love down upon the world.

———— ⟨⟩ ————

"Oh, my God!" I cried in the depths of my heart, "will it only be your justice that will receive souls that offer themselves as sacrificial victims? Doesn't your merciful love need them as well? Everywhere it is misunderstood, rejected. The hearts into which you desire to pour it are turned toward created things, asking them for happiness with their wretched affection, instead of throwing themselves into your arms and accepting your infinite love.

"Oh, my God! Meeting with such contempt, is your love going to remain in your heart? It seems to me that if you found souls that were offering themselves as sacrificial victims to your love, you would consume them rapidly. It seems to me that you would be happy not to dam up the waves of infinite tenderness that are within you.

"If your justice, which extends only over the earth, likes to vent itself, how much more does your merciful love desire to set souls on fire, since your mercy rises all the way to heaven [Psalm 36:5].

"Oh, my Jesus! Let me be that happy victim; consume your sacrifice through the fire of your divine love!" (SS Edmonson 204–5)

Thérèse received permission from her mother superior, whom she addresses here, to offer herself as a victim of God's love. Although she was destined to endure intense suffering, she never regretted her decision.

Beloved Mother, you who have allowed me to offer myself in this way to God, you know the rivers or rather the oceans of graces that have come to flood my soul.

Oh! Since that happy day, it seems to me that love penetrates and surrounds me. It seems to me that at every moment that merciful love is renewing me, purifying my soul, and leaving there no trace of sin, so I cannot fear purgatory.

I know that in myself I wouldn't be worthy even to enter that place of expiation, since only holy souls can have access to it, but I also know that the fire of love is more sanctifying than that of purgatory.

Oh! How sweet is the path of love! How I want to apply myself to always doing, with the greatest abandonment, the will of God [Matthew 6:10]! (SS Edmonson 205–6)

When Thérèse offered herself to God's love, she experienced an overwhelming mystical sign of his acceptance. She described the moment for her sister Marie.

I was beginning the Way of the Cross; suddenly, I was seized with such a violent love for God that I can't explain it except by saying it felt as though I were totally plunged into fire. Oh! What fire and what sweetness at one and the same time! I was on fire with love and I felt that one minute more, one second more, and I wouldn't be able to sustain this ardor without dying.

I understood, then, what the saints were saying about these states which they experienced so often. . . . I experienced it only once and for one single instant, falling back immediately into my habitual state of dryness. (HLC 77)

How sweet is the path of love. No doubt, one can fall down, one can commit unfaithful acts, but love, knowing how to profit from everything, quickly consumes everything that can be displeasing to Jesus, leaving only a humble and profound peace in the depths of the heart. (SS Edmonson 202)

God's Justice—an Aspect of His Love

God's justice, Thérèse said, is simply another aspect of his love. We need not fear it, since it flows from his infinite compassion for his children.

I know one must be very pure to appear before the God of all holiness, but I know, too, that the Lord is infinitely just; and it is this justice which frightens so many souls that is the object of my joy and confidence.

To be just is not only to exercise severity in order to punish the guilty; it is also to recognize right intentions and to reward virtue. I expect as much from God's justice as from his mercy.

It is because he is just that "He is compassionate and filled with gentleness, slow to punish, and abundant in mercy, for he knows our frailty, he remembers we are only dust. As a father has tenderness for his children, so the Lord has compassion on us" [Psalm 103:8-13]. (GC II 1093)

After so many graces can I not sing with the psalmist, "For the Lord is good and his love endures forever"? [Psalm 100:5].

It seems to me that if all creatures had the same graces as I, God would be feared by no one, but loved passionately, and that out of love and not out of trembling [in fear], no soul would ever consent to cause him grief.

I understand, however, that all souls can't look alike. There have to be some from different families in order to especially honor each of God's perfections.

To me he's given his infinite mercy, and it's through it that I contemplate and adore the other divine perfections! Then all of them appear to me radiant with love. Righteousness and justice themselves (and perhaps even more than any other perfections) seem to me to be clothed in love.

What sweet joy it is to think that God is just—that is, that he takes into account our weakness, he knows perfectly the fragility of our nature. What should I be afraid of? Oh! The infinitely just God who deigned to forgive with such kindness all the faults of the prodigal son [Luke 15:21-24], should he not also be just toward me who am "always with him"? [Luke 15:31]. (SS Edmonson 203–4)

To Love Jesus with Passion

One night, not knowing how to tell Jesus that I loved him and how much I desired that he be everywhere loved and glorified, I was thinking with sorrow that he could never receive in hell a single act of love. So I told God that to please him I would willingly consent to find myself plunged into hell, so that he might be eternally loved in that place of blasphemy.

I knew that that couldn't glorify him, since he desires only our happiness, but when one loves, one experiences the need to say a thousand foolish things. If I spoke that way, it wasn't because heaven excited my desire, but that my personal heaven was none other than love, and I felt like St. Paul that nothing could separate me from the divine object that had stolen my heart [Romans 8:35-39]! (SS Edmonson 122–23)

All the great truths of religion, the mysteries of eternity, plunged my soul into a happiness that was not of earth [I Corinthians 2:9]. I was already feeling what God reserves for those who love him (not with the human eye, but with that of the heart), and seeing that eternal rewards have no proportion to the slight sacrifices of life [2 Corinthians 4:17], I wanted to love, love Jesus with passion, give him a thousand signs of love while I could still do it. (SS Edmonson 109)

Thinking Only of God's Pleasure

It was the custom of the Carmelites for each sister to compose a letter to the Lord and to carry it with her when she made her vows. Thérèse's letter encompasses many of her virtues, such as humility and zeal, but it was motivated by her immense love for God.

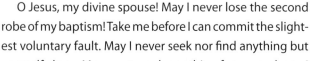

O Jesus, my divine spouse! May I never lose the second robe of my baptism! Take me before I can commit the slightest voluntary fault. May I never seek nor find anything but yourself alone. May creatures be nothing for me and may I be nothing for them, but may you, Jesus, be everything!

May the things of earth never be able to trouble my soul, and may nothing disturb my peace. Jesus, I ask you for nothing but peace, and also love, infinite love without any limits other than yourself; love which is no longer I but you, my Jesus.

Jesus, may I die a martyr for you. Give me martyrdom of heart or of body, or rather give me both. Give me the grace to fulfill my vows in all their perfection, and make me understand what a real spouse of yours should be.

Let me never be a burden to the community, let nobody be occupied with me, let me be looked upon as one to be trampled underfoot, forgotten like your little grain of sand, Jesus.

May your will be done in me perfectly, and may I arrive at the place you have prepared for me.

Jesus, allow me to save very many souls; let no soul be lost today; let all the souls in purgatory be saved. Jesus, pardon me if I say anything I should not say. I want only to give you joy and to console you. (SS Clarke 275)

Many serve Jesus when he is consoling them, but few consent to keep company with Jesus sleeping on the waves or suffering in the garden of agony! Who, then, will be willing to serve Jesus for himself! (GC II 862)

I know no other means of reaching perfection but (love). Love, how well our heart is made for that! Sometimes, I seek for another word to express love, but on this earth of exile words are powerless to express all the soul's vibrations, so we have to keep to this one word: (love!). (GC I 641)

It is easy to please Jesus, to enrapture his heart; you have only to love him, without looking at yourselves, without spending too much time examining your own faults. (STL 135)

Take Jesus by the Heart

One of her fellow nuns said that Thérèse's love for God was like that of a child's love for her father and that she expressed this love in surprising ways. Here, Thérèse speaks with her customary simplicity and confidence.

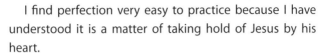

I find perfection very easy to practice because I have understood it is a matter of taking hold of Jesus by his heart.

Look at a little child who has just annoyed his mother by flying into a temper or by disobeying her. If he hides away in a corner in a sulky mood and if he cries in fear of being punished, his mamma will not pardon him. . . . But if he comes to her, holding out his little arms, smiling, and saying: "Kiss me, I will not do it again," will his mother be able not to press him to her heart tenderly and forget his childish mischief?

However, she knows her dear little one will do it again on the next occasion, but this does not matter; if he takes her again by her heart, he will not be punished. (GC II 965–66)

Do not fear to tell [Jesus] you love him, even without feeling it. This is the way to force Jesus to help you, to carry you like a little child too feeble to walk. (GC II 1117)

Abandonment to His Will

On a practical level, Thérèse's love for God found expression in her complete acceptance of his will. This abandonment guided everything she did, from accepting suffering to faithfully carrying out her duties.

This saying of Job: "Although he should kill me, I will trust in him" [Job 13:15]; has fascinated me from my childhood. But it took me a long time before I was established in this degree of abandonment. Now I am there; God has placed me there. He took me into his arms and placed me there. (HLC 77)

My heart is filled with God's will, and when someone pours something on it, this doesn't penetrate its interior; it's a nothing which glides off easily, just like oil which can't mix with water. I remain always at profound peace in the depths of my heart; nothing can disturb it. (HLC 97)

All is well when we seek only the will of Jesus. (SS Edmonson 229)

The only happiness on earth is to apply oneself in always finding delightful the lot Jesus is giving us. (GC II 1148–49)

The Folly of Divine Love

In a letter to Céline, Thérèse comments on the folly of divine love.

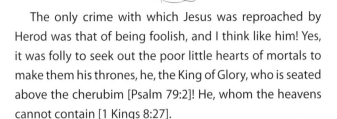

The only crime with which Jesus was reproached by Herod was that of being foolish, and I think like him! Yes, it was folly to seek out the poor little hearts of mortals to make them his thrones, he, the King of Glory, who is seated above the cherubim [Psalm 79:2]! He, whom the heavens cannot contain [1 Kings 8:27].

He was foolish, our beloved, to come to earth in search of sinners in order to make them his friends, his intimates, his equals, he who was perfectly happy with the two adorable persons of the Trinity!

We shall never be able to carry out the follies he carried out for us . . . for they are only very rational acts and much below what our love would like to accomplish.

It is the world, then, that is senseless since it does not know what Jesus has done to save it, it is the world which is a monopolizer, which seduces souls, and which leads them to springs without water [Jeremiah 2:13]. (GC II 882)

Reflection

Many of us grapple with fear in our lives—fear of sin, fear of suffering, fear of death, fear of failure, fear of war, fear that our sins will be found out. The list is endless. We live in an atmosphere of dread that is incompatible with the gospel and undermines our faith.

Thérèse was not afraid of anything. She loved God, he loved her, and that was enough. The same can be true for us if we take God at his word and believe the good news. "Perfect love casts out fear" (1 John 4:18).

Prayer

Lord, I know I don't grasp the depth of your love for me. Free me from everything that holds me back from receiving you. Let me love you without fear, knowing that you hold me in the palm of your hand. Through Christ our Lord, Amen.

Chapter Two

THE COST OF LOVING ONE'S NEIGHBOR

G. K. Chesterton once said of St. Francis of Assisi: "He was a lover of God and he was really and truly a lover of men, possibly a much rarer mystical vocation."[1] The same is true of Thérèse of Lisieux.

Thérèse loved God passionately, as we might expect of a nun in a cloistered convent. But she loved her neighbor with equal zeal, a more difficult virtue to sustain. Far from isolating her, convent life was in some ways a more intense experience of ordinary life: difficult personalities and petty problems were literally inescapable within the confines of the cloister.

She tackled the situation with her customary determination. Everything we do is worthless unless we do it with love, Thérèse said flatly. To dispel any illusions about the cost involved, she added that only the entire sacrifice of oneself can be classified as real love.

Thérèse made that sacrifice to an extraordinary degree in the very ordinary circumstances of daily life. On some level, however, anybody can do what she did, as the excerpts in this chapter illustrate.

Thérèse insisted that if we take the first step, God will give us the grace necessary to love those around us. Often this means nothing more than offering a kind word or a helping hand when we don't feel like it.

Initially, Thérèse herself found such small challenges difficult. She struggled, and the effort showed on her face. With practice, though, self-sacrifice came much more easily. And each time she made good use of the grace God gave her to conquer herself, she claimed, he gave her yet more grace. Still, she noted that there were occasions when she had to take her courage in both hands in order to avoid snapping at someone.

Thérèse recognized that love of neighbor is an essential ingredient of the gospel, however impossible the task may seem. She never implied that it would be easy. At times, in fact, she practiced the virtue as a sort of martyrdom. Still, she stuck with it, and she urged others to do the same.

Thérèse found support for her tenacity in one of her favorite quotes from St. John of the Cross: "The smallest movement of pure love is more useful to the church than all other works put together."

The Jesus in Others

From time to time, most of us find ourselves in situations with someone whose appearance or speech or personality irritate us. One particular nun had this effect on Thérèse. Here's how she handled it.

———————

Not wishing to give in to the natural antipathy I was experiencing, I told myself that charity must not consist in feelings but in works; then I set myself to doing for this sister what I would do for the person I loved the most. Each time I met her I prayed to God for her, offering him all her virtues and merits. . . .

I wasn't content simply with praying very much for this sister who gave me so many struggles, but I took care to render her all the services possible, and when I was tempted to answer her back in a disagreeable manner, I was content with giving her my most friendly smile, and with changing the subject of the conversation, for *The Imitation [of Christ]* says: "It is better to leave each one in his own opinion than to enter into arguments."

Frequently, when I was not at recreation . . . and had occasion to work with this sister, I used to run away like a deserter whenever my struggles became too violent. As she was absolutely unaware of my feelings for her, never did she suspect the motives for my conduct and she remained convinced that her character was very pleasing to me.

One day at recreation she asked in almost these words: "Would you tell me, Sister Thérèse of the Child Jesus, what attracts you so much towards me; every time you look at me, I see you smile?"

Ah! What attracted me was Jesus hidden in the depths of her soul; Jesus who makes sweet what is most bitter. I answered that I was smiling because I was happy to see her (it is understood that I did not add that this was from a spiritual standpoint). (SS Clarke 222–23)

The most trivial work, the least action when inspired by love, is often of greater merit than the most outstanding achievement. It is not on their face value that God judges our deeds, even when they bear the stamp of apparent holiness, but solely on the measure of love we put into them. (MSST 74)

Thérèse noticed how the infirmarian always had soft, fresh linens on hand for the comfort of the sick nuns in the infirmary.

Souls should be treated with the same tender care, but why is it that we forget this so frequently, and allow those about us to go on unnoticed in the endurance of sharp, interior pain? Shouldn't the spiritual needs of the soul be attended to with the same charity, with the same delicate care which we devote to our neighbor's bodily necessities?

For some souls are really sick; there are many weak souls on earth, and all souls without exception suffer at one time or other during life. How tenderly we should not only love them but also show our love for them. (MSST 130–31)

It Didn't Come Easily

Love of neighbor didn't come easily to Thérèse. She had to work at it, just like the rest of us. Her intense determination to conquer herself and love those around her, however, sets her apart from the ordinary Christian. This simple example should strike a chord with anyone who has ever had to endure the whispering of others at church, a concert, or a movie.

———

For a long time at evening meditation, I was placed in front of a sister who had a strange habit. . . . As soon as this sister arrived, she began making a strange little noise which resembled the noise one would make when rubbing two shells, one against the other. I was the only one to notice it because I had extremely sensitive hearing (too much so at times). . . .

It would be impossible for me to tell you how much this little noise wearied me. I had a great desire to turn my head and stare at the culprit who was certainly very unaware of her "click." This would be the only way of enlightening her. However, in the bottom of my heart I felt it was much better to suffer this out of love for God and not to cause the sister any pain. I remained calm, therefore, and tried to unite myself to God and to forget the little noise.

Everything was useless. I felt the perspiration inundate me, and I was obliged simply to make a prayer of suffering; however, while suffering, I searched for a way of doing it without annoyance and with peace and joy, at least in the interior of my soul. I tried to love the little noise which was so displeasing; instead of trying not to hear it (impossible), I paid close attention so as to hear it well, as though it were a delightful concert, and my prayer (which was not the prayer of quiet) was spent in offering this concert to Jesus. (SS Clarke 249–50)

Charity consists in bearing with the faults of others, in not being surprised at their weakness, in being edified by the smallest acts of virtue we see them practice. (SS Clarke 220)

When . . . the devil tries to place before the eyes of my soul the faults of such and such a sister . . . I hasten to search out her virtues, her good intentions; I tell myself that even if I did see her fall once, she could easily have won a great number of victories which she is hiding through humility, and that even what appears to me as a fault can very easily be an act of virtue because of her intention. (SS Clarke 221)

Befriending the Imperfect

In the Gospel of Luke, Jesus tells his followers to take special care of the needy. "When you give a luncheon or a dinner, do not invite your friends . . . in case they may invite you in return, and you would be repaid. But when you give a banquet, invite the poor, the crippled, the lame, and the blind" (Luke 14:12-13).

Thérèse applied these words to some of her fellow nuns who, for one reason or another, had difficult personalities. Her approach is a striking example of the gospel in action.

I've noticed (and it's quite natural) that the holiest sisters are the most loved. People seek out their conversation, and they render services to them without their asking for them. . . .

Imperfect souls, on the other hand, are not sought out. No doubt people remain on their behalf within the boundaries of religious politeness, but perhaps out of fear of saying some not-so-nice words to them, people avoid their company.

By saying "imperfect souls," I don't mean to speak only about spiritual imperfections, since the holiest of persons will be perfect only in heaven. I mean to speak about the lack of judgment, of manners, of susceptibility in certain characters—all the things that don't make life very pleasant. I know well that these moral infirmities are chronic. There's no hope of cure....

Here's the conclusion that I make from this: I must seek out during recreation periods, during free time, the company of the sisters who are the least pleasant to me, and fulfill among those blessed souls the role of the Good Samaritan. One word, one pleasant smile, are often enough to cause a sad soul to brighten up.

But it's not absolutely to attain that goal that I want to practice charity, because I know that soon I would be discouraged: a word that I might have said with the best of intentions might perhaps be interpreted all wrong. Therefore, so as not to waste my time, I want to be pleasant with everyone (and particularly with the least pleasant sisters) in order to give joy to Jesus. (SS Edmonson 279–80)

Love, Above All Else

Thérèse had been ordered by her superiors to write her autobiography. As her illness progressed, this became physically difficult. The constant interruptions of the other nuns, however, proved more of a trial than her dwindling strength. Parents of young children—indeed, anyone subjected to frequent interruptions—can identify with Thérèse's dilemma.

Her solution? Love, above all else. Thérèse simply put aside what she was doing and gave each sister her undivided attention.

Her dry sense of humor is apparent as she describes a typical day. Thérèse is sitting in the garden in a wheelchair while the other nuns bring in the hay.

When I begin to take up my pen, behold a sister who passes by, a pitchfork on her shoulder. She believes she will distract me with a little idle chatter: hay, ducks, hens, visits of the doctor, everything is discussed; to tell the truth, this doesn't last a long time, but there is more than one good charitable sister, and all of a sudden another hay worker throws flowers on my lap, perhaps believing these will inspire me with poetic thoughts. I am not looking for them at the moment and would prefer to see the flowers remain swaying on their stems. . . .

I don't know if I have been able to write ten lines without being disturbed; . . . however, for the love of God and my sisters (so charitable towards me) I take care to appear happy and especially to be so.

For example, here is a hay worker who is just leaving me after having said very compassionately: "Poor little sister, it must tire you out writing like that all day long" "Don't worry," I answer, "I appear to be writing very much, but really I am writing almost nothing." "Very good!" she says, "but just the same, I am very happy we are doing the haying since this always distracts you a little."

In fact, it is such a great distraction for me . . . that I am not telling any lies when I say that I am writing practically nothing. (SS Clarke 227–28)

Ah! What peace floods the soul when she rises above natural feelings. (SS Clarke 226)

Thérèse wanted to be everything for the Lord— a martyr, a priest, a saint, a missionary, an evangelist. Tormented by these unfulfilled longings, she sought an answer in the epistles of Paul. In 1 Corinthians 12 she read that the church has many members performing a variety of functions; not all can be prophets or apostles or evangelists.

That was a clear answer, but it failed to provide a focus for her yearnings. Reading on, she came upon Paul's famous passage on love in 1 Corinthians 13. At last, Thérèse felt she had found the key to her vocation.

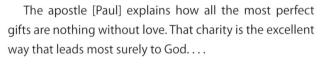

The apostle [Paul] explains how all the most perfect gifts are nothing without love. That charity is the excellent way that leads most surely to God. . . .

I finally had rest. Considering the mystical body of the church, I had not recognized myself in any of the members described by St. Paul, or rather I desired to see myself in them all. Charity gave me the key to my vocation.

I understood that if the church had a body composed of different members, the most necessary and most noble of all could not be lacking to it, and so I understood that the church had a heart and that this heart was burning with love.

I understood it was love alone that made the church's members act, that if love ever became extinct, apostles would not preach the gospel and martyrs would not shed their blood.

I understood that love comprised all vocations, that love was everything, that it embraced all times and places, in a word, that it was eternal. . . .

I cried out: O Jesus, my love, my vocation, at last I have found it. My vocation is love!

Yes, I have found my place in the church and it is you, O my God, who have given me this place; in the heart of the church, . . . I shall be love. Thus I shall be everything, and thus my dream will be realized. (SS Clarke 194)

When the Lord commanded his people to love their neighbor as themselves, he had not as yet come upon the earth. Knowing the extent to which each one loved himself, he was not able to ask of his creatures a greater love than this for one's neighbor.

But when Jesus gave his apostles a new commandment, his own commandment as he calls it later on [John 15:12], it is no longer a question of loving one's neighbor as oneself but of loving him as he, Jesus, has loved him, and will love him till the consummation of the ages.

Ah! Lord, I know that you don't command the impossible. You know better than I do my weakness and imperfection; you know very well that never would I be able to love my sisters as you love them, unless you, O my Jesus, loved them in me. It is because you wanted to give me this grace that you made your new commandment. Oh! How I love this new commandment since it gives me the assurance that your will is to love in me all those you command me to love!

Yes, I feel it, when I am charitable, it is Jesus alone who is acting in me, and the more I am united to him, the more also do I love my sisters. (SS Clarke 220–21)

Loving the Unlovable

Sister St. Pierre, an elderly invalid, needed help every evening to get from church to the dining room. She was hard to please, so no one was eager to volunteer. Thérèse offered to help her, remembering the words of the gospel: "As often as you did it for one of my least brothers, you did it for me" (Matthew 25:40).

Each evening when I saw Sister St. Pierre shake her hour-glass I knew this meant: "Let's go!" It is incredible how difficult it was for me to get up, especially at the beginning; however, I did it immediately, and then a ritual was set in motion. I had to remove and carry her little bench in a certain way, above all I was not to hurry, and then the walk took place.

It was a question of following the poor invalid by holding her cincture; I did this with as much gentleness as possible. But if by mistake she took a false step, immediately it appeared to her that I was holding her incorrectly and that she was about to fall. "Ah, my God! You are going too fast; I'm going to break something."

If I tried to go more slowly: "Well, come on! I don't feel your hand; you've let me go and I'm going to fall! Ah! I was right when I said you were too young to help me."

Finally, we reached the refectory without mishap; and here other difficulties arose. I had to seat Sister St. Pierre and I had to act skillfully in order not to hurt her; then I had to turn back her sleeves (again in a certain way), and afterwards I was free to leave.

With her poor crippled hands she was trying to manage with her bread as well as she could. I soon noticed this, and, each evening, I did not leave her until after I had rendered her this little service. As she had not asked for this, she was very much touched by my attention, and it was by this means that I gained her entire good graces, and this especially (I learned this later) because, after cutting her bread for her, I gave her my most beautiful smile." (SS Clarke 247–48)

Generosity of the Heart

Thérèse felt that there should be no limits to generosity. She pointed out, however, that the attitude of the giver is even more important than the act of giving.

———————— ⤳ ————————

Our Lord said again, "And if you lend to those from whom you expect repayment, what credit is that to you? Even sinners lend to sinners, expecting to be repaid in full. But . . . do good . . . and lend . . . without expecting to get anything back. Then your reward will be great" [Luke 6:34-35].

Oh, yes! The reward is great even on earth. . . . When we follow that road it's only the first step that costs us.

To lend without expecting to get anything back seems hard to our nature. We would prefer to give, because some thing we give doesn't belong to us any more. When someone comes and tells us with a convincing look, "Sister, I need your help for a few hours. But don't worry, I have permission from our Superior, and I'll pay back the time that you're giving me, because I know how pressed for time you are."

In truth, when we know quite well that the time we lend will never be paid back, we'd rather say, "I give it to you." That would make our self-love happy, because giving is a more generous act than lending, and then we make the sister feel that we're not counting on her to do something for us.

Oh! How contrary Jesus' teachings are to the thoughts of nature. Without the help of his grace it would be impossible not only to put them into practice, but even more to understand them. (SS Edmonson 259–60)

As she lay dying, Thérèse had firsthand experience of the importance of generous care for the sick.

Pray for the poor sick who are dying. If you only knew what happens! How little it takes to lose one's patience! You must be kind towards all of them without exception. I would not have believed this formerly! (HLC 130)

How easy it is to become discouraged when we are very sick! Oh, how I sense that I'd become discouraged if I didn't have any faith! Or at least if I didn't love God! (HLC 132)

Reflection

Scripture says that we are created in the image and likeness of God. C. S. Lewis arrived at a reasonable conclusion, then, when he said in *The Weight of Glory* that our neighbor is the holiest object we encounter, next to the Blessed Sacrament itself.

The fact is that we more often treat those around us as inconsequential than as holy. People can be irritating and mean tempered, and our instinctive reaction is to respond in kind. Thérèse felt the same impulse, but, clinging to the gospel, she returned good for evil.

Thérèse points out that love of neighbor is a matter of choice and the grace of God. The choice is up to us, and Thérèse is confident that God will supply the grace. She doesn't say it will be easy, but she insists that, if we are to follow the gospel, it is essential. "This I command you, to love one another" (John 15:17).

Prayer

Lord, nothing you ask me to do seems as difficult as loving my neighbor. Give me the strength not only to love when my neighbor is most unlovable, but to find joy in doing so. Prevent me from giving way to the impatience and anger that wounds others. Help me to act on the knowledge that we are all created in your image. Through Christ our Lord, Amen.

1. G. K. Chesterton, *St. Francis of Assisi* (Garden City, NY: Doubleday Image Books, 1989), 7.

Chapter Three

EMBRACING SUFFERING

Most people do their best to avoid suffering. Not Thérèse of Lisieux. In fact, she was so drawn to suffering that she said she felt it was a "magnet" that drew her to itself. She felt a real thirst for it, she said on one occasion; and, on another, she stated that she wanted only one thing and that was to always suffer for Jesus.

Readers who are enthusiastic over Thérèse's Little Way begin to have their doubts when they encounter material such as this. Ordinary life brings as much pain as most people can handle. Who needs a saint who thirsts for more?

Was Thérèse psychologically disturbed? Did she have a morbid interest in pain? In this regard, she's not particularly appealing to a culture caught up in the pursuit of happiness and material possessions.

On the other hand, perhaps Thérèse simply discovered and laid bare a truth implicit in the gospel: that suffering is redemptive and can draw us closer to God. This, in fact, is her point. She had as her model Jesus himself, the Suffering Servant who chose his Father's will above his own.

Thérèse had no interest in suffering for its own sake. She chose to embrace it for two reasons. First, she wanted God to know that her love for him was completely free of self-interest. In other words, she didn't love him for the blessings or consolations he might send her way, but simply for himself.

In fact, he sent her very few consolations. Her prayer life was barren, her daily life was one of continual sacrifice, and she endured tremendous spiritual and physical pain throughout the year before she died. She handled it all with confident trust in God's faithfulness.

Second, and just as important, she offered up her suffering for the conversion of sinners. She noted that she wasn't called to Carmel for her own happiness but to lay down her life for others and to bring sinners to heaven. She was a mother of souls, she said, and her work would be done in sorrow.

In spite of the role suffering plays in Thérèse's spirituality, she was cautious about asking God to send some her way. "If I were to ask for sufferings," she said, "these would be mine and I would have to bear them alone and I've never been able to do anything alone" (HLC 145).

As Thérèse matured, she actually focused less on suffering and more on conformity to God's will, with whatever suffering that entailed.

Thérèse's approach to pain is simply the Christian approach, heightened by her ardent love for God and her intense desire to save souls. Further, the pain that Thérèse most often speaks of is the deep interior suffering that accompanies dying to self. This is nothing more than the cost of following the gospel. Embrace this, Thérèse says, and not only will you grow in holiness, but your suffering will serve as a prayer on behalf of sinners.

Martyrdom of the Heart: Interior Suffering

True courage does not consist in those momentary ardors which impel us to go out and win the world to Christ—at the cost of every imaginable danger, which only adds another touch of romance to our beautiful dreams.

No, the courage that counts with God is that type of courage which our Lord showed in the Garden of Olives: on the one hand, a natural desire to turn away from suffering; on the other, in anguish of soul the willing acceptance of the chalice which his Father had sent him. (MSST 191)

In a letter to Céline, Thérèse provides a glimpse into the extent of her interior suffering. Her habitual lack of consolation in prayer and her sense of distance from God seem like martyrdom to her.

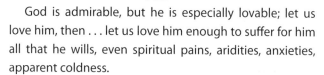

God is admirable, but he is especially lovable; let us love him, then . . . let us love him enough to suffer for him all that he wills, even spiritual pains, aridities, anxieties, apparent coldness.

Ah, here is great love, to love Jesus without feeling the sweetness of this love . . . this is martyrdom. . . . Unknown martyrdom, known to God alone, which the eye of the creature cannot discover, a martyrdom without honor, without triumph. That is love pushed to the point of heroism.

But, one day, a grateful God will cry out: "Now, my turn." Oh, what will we see then? What is this life which will no more have an end? God will be the soul of our soul . . . unfathomable mystery. . . .

The eye of man has not seen the uncreated light, his ear has not heard the incomparable harmonies, and his heart cannot have any idea of what God reserves for those whom he loves [1 Corinthians 2:9]. (GC I 577)

Trials help very much in detaching us from this earth. They make us look higher than this world. Here below, nothing can satisfy us. We cannot enjoy a little rest except in being ready to do God's will. (GC I 400)

Shortly after Thérèse's first Communion, her sister Marie spoke to her about suffering. She told Thérèse that God would probably not allow her to suffer much but would carry her through life as a child. Thérèse thought about that and came to a different conclusion.

———

I felt born within my heart a great desire to suffer, and at the same time the interior assurance that Jesus reserved a great number of crosses for me. I felt myself flooded with consolations so great that I look upon them as one of the greatest graces of my life.

Suffering became my attraction. . . . Up until this time, I had suffered without loving suffering, but since this day I felt a real love for it. I also felt the desire of loving only God, of finding my joy only in him.

Often during my Communions, I repeated these words of *The Imitation [of Christ]*: "O Jesus, unspeakable sweetness, change all the consolations of this earth into bitterness for me!" (SS Clarke 79)

When you want to reach a goal, you must use every means to do so. Jesus made me understand that it was by the cross that he wanted to give me souls, and my drawing toward suffering grew in proportion to the suffering that was increasing. (SS Edmonson 169)

My desire for suffering was answered, and yet my attraction for it did not diminish. My soul soon shared in the sufferings of my heart. Spiritual aridity was my daily bread and, deprived of all consolation, I was still the happiest of creatures since all my desires had been satisfied. (SS Clarke 157)

I desire only one thing when I am in Carmel; it is always . . . to suffer for Jesus. Life passes so quickly that truly it must be better to have a very beautiful crown [in heaven] and a little trouble than (not) to have an ordinary one without any trouble. . . . In suffering, one can save souls. (GC I 399)

Sanctity does not consist in saying beautiful things, it does not even consist in thinking them, in feeling them! It consists in suffering and suffering everything. (Sanctity! We must conquer it at the point of the sword; we must suffer . . . we must agonize!) (GC I 557–58)

It is so sweet to serve our Lord in the night of trial; we have only this life to practice the virtue of faith. (MSST 197)

A Dark Night of the Soul

During the last year and a half of her life, Thérèse struggled with temptations to despair, to fear that God didn't love her, that heaven didn't exist, and that she was eternally damned. She said that she could understand the temptation to suicide (HLC 196, 258, 295).

This assault on her faith came unexpectedly and lasted until her death. Her suffering was extreme, but she endured, making her an inspiring model for those who deal with similar doubts and fears. The next excerpts are from this period of her life.

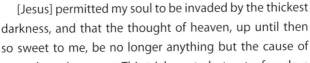

[Jesus] permitted my soul to be invaded by the thickest darkness, and that the thought of heaven, up until then so sweet to me, be no longer anything but the cause of struggle and torment. This trial was to last not a few days or a few weeks, it was not to be extinguished until the hour set by God himself and this hour has not yet come.

I would like to be able to express what I feel, but alas! I believe this is impossible. One would have to travel through this dark tunnel to understand it's darkness....

When I want to rest my heart fatigued by the darkness which surrounds it by the memory of the luminous country [heaven] after which I aspire, my torment redoubles; it seems to me that the darkness, borrowing the voice of sinners, says mockingly to me: "You are dreaming about the light ... you are dreaming about the eternal possession of the Creator; ... you believe that one day you will walk out of this fog which surrounds you! Advance, advance; rejoice in death which will give you not what you hope for but a night still more profound, the night of nothingness."

The image . . . of the darkness that obscures my soul is as imperfect as a sketch is to the model; however, I don't want to write any longer about it; I fear I might blaspheme; I fear even that I have already said too much.

Ah! May Jesus pardon me if I have caused him any pain, but he knows very well that while I do not have the joy of faith, I am trying to carry out its works at least. I believe I have made more acts of faith in this past year than all through my whole life. (SS Clarke 211–13)

Although Thérèse was troubled about the reality of heaven, she faced this dark night of the soul with courage and joy. Addressing herself to her mother superior, she explains how she met this spiritual assault.

———————

I conduct myself bravely. . . . I run toward my Jesus, I tell him that I'm ready to shed my blood even to the last drop in order to confess that there is a heaven. I tell him that I'm happy not to enjoy that beautiful heaven on earth in order that he might open it for eternity to the poor unbelievers.

So, despite this trial that's taking away all enjoyment, I can nonetheless cry out, "For you make me glad by your deeds, LORD" [Psalm 92:4]. For, is there a greater gladness than that of suffering out of love for you?

The more private the suffering is, the less evident it is to the eyes of created beings, the more it makes you glad, God. But if, against all possibility, you yourself were not to know of my suffering, I would still be happy to possess it, if by it I could prevent or make reparation for a single fault committed against the faith. . . .

I may perhaps seem to you to be exaggerating my trial. In fact, if you judge according to the sentiments that I express in the little poems that I've composed this year, I must seem to you to be a soul filled with consolations and for whom the veil of faith has almost torn open, and yet . . . it's no longer a veil for me, it's a wall that rises up to heaven and covers the starry sky.

When I sing of the happiness of heaven, the everlasting possession of God, I feel no joy because of it, because I simply sing of what I want to believe. (SS Edmonson 238–39)

During the last year of her life, Thérèse was surprised by the extent of her physical and spiritual suffering. She didn't expect to suffer like this, she said, and her anguish and doubts are evident as she struggles to accept the challenge.

I wonder how God can hold himself back for such a long time from taking me. And then, one would say that he wants to make me believe that there is no heaven!

And all the saints whom I love so much, where are they "hanging out"?

Ah! I'm not pretending, it's very true that I don't see a thing. But I must sing very strongly in my heart: "After death life is immortal," or without this, things would turn out badly. (HLC 150)

The angels can't suffer; therefore, they are not as fortunate as I am. How astonished they would be if they suffered and felt what I feel! Yes, they'd be very surprised because so am I myself. (HLC 150)

If you only knew what frightful thoughts obsess me! Pray very much for me in order that I do not listen to the devil who wants to persuade me about so many lies. It's the reasoning of the worst materialists which is imposed upon my mind: Later, unceasingly, making new advances, science will explain everything naturally; we shall have the absolute reason for everything that exists and that still remains a problem, because there remain very many things to be discovered, etc., etc.

I want to do good after my death, but I will not be able to do so! It will be as it was for Mother Geneviève [the founder of the Lisieux Carmel]; We expected to see her work miracles, and complete silence fell over her tomb....

Must one have thoughts like this when one loves God so much! Finally, I offer up these very great pains to obtain the light of faith for poor unbelievers, for all those who separate themselves from the church's beliefs.

I undergo [thoughts like these] under duress, but while undergoing them I never cease making acts of faith. (HLC 257)

Looking out her window, Thérèse pointed to a shady part of the garden and said,

Do you see the black hole [she was pointing to the chestnut trees near the cemetery] where we can see nothing; it's in a similar hole that I am as far as body and soul are concerned. Ah! What darkness! But I am in peace. (HLC 173)

God gives me courage in proportion to my sufferings. I feel at this moment I couldn't suffer any more, but I'm not afraid, since if they increase, he will increase my courage at the same time. (HLC 149)

Inner Conflict Caused by Aridity and Pain

Sometimes when we are suffering, people ignore our pain and expect us to be upbeat. Thérèse had a similar experience. One of the sisters came into the infirmary every night, stood at the foot of Thérèse's bed, and laughed and smiled inanely, apparently under the impression she was cheering the patient up. Here's how Thérèse handled this irritating behavior.

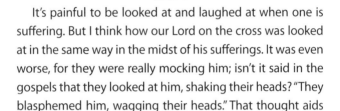

It's painful to be looked at and laughed at when one is suffering. But I think how our Lord on the cross was looked at in the same way in the midst of his sufferings. It was even worse, for they were really mocking him; isn't it said in the gospels that they looked at him, shaking their heads? "They blasphemed him, wagging their heads." That thought aids me in offering him this sacrifice in the right spirit. (HLC 167)

In this letter to Céline, Thérèse reveals some of her conflicting thoughts about the aridity and pain that she endures.

Life is burdensome. What bitterness . . . but what sweetness. Yes, life is painful for us. It is hard to begin a day of work. . . . If we feel Jesus present, oh! then we would really do all for him, but no, he seems a thousand leagues away. We are all alone with ourselves. . . . What annoying company when Jesus is not there.

But what is this sweet Friend doing then? Doesn't he see our anguish, the weight that is oppressing us? Where is he? Why doesn't he come to console us since we have him alone for a friend?

Alas, he is not far; he is there, very close. He is looking at us, and he is begging this sorrow, this agony from us. He needs it for souls [as an offering for sinners] and for our soul. He wants to give us such a beautiful recompense, and his ambitions for us are very great.

But how can he say: "My turn," if ours hasn't come, if we have given him nothing? Alas, it does pain him to give us sorrows to drink, but he knows this is the only means of preparing us to "know him as he knows himself and to become gods ourselves" [1 Corinthians 13:12]. Oh! What a destiny. How great is our soul.

Let us raise ourselves above what is passing away. Let us keep ourselves a distance from the earth. Higher up the air is pure. Jesus is hiding himself, but we can see him. . . .

I read this morning a passage of the gospel where it says: "I have not come to bring peace but the sword" [Matthew 10:34]. There remains nothing else for us to do but to fight, and when we don't have the strength, it is then that Jesus fights for us. (GC I 449–50)

Weary but Unwavering

Thérèse's weariness coupled with her determination are evident in this letter to Céline.

I have a need this evening . . . to forget this earth. Here below, everything tires me, everything is a burden to me. I find only one joy, that of suffering for Jesus. . . .

Life is passing away. Eternity is advancing in great strides. Soon we shall live the very life of Jesus. After having drunk at the fountain of all sorrows, we shall be deified at the very fountain of all joys, all delights. . . .

"The image of this world is passing away" [1 Corinthians 7:31]. Soon we shall see new heavens. . . . Immensity will be our domain. We shall no longer be prisoners on this earth of exile. All will have passed away! With our heavenly spouse, we shall sail on lakes without any shores. . . . (Courage, Jesus can hear the very last echo of our sorrow.)

Our harps, at this moment, are hung on the willows which border the river of Babylon [Psalm 86:2]. But on the day of our deliverance, what songs will be heard, . . . with what joy shall we make the strings of our instruments vibrate!

Love is repaid by love alone, and the wounds of love are healed only by love. Let us really offer our sufferings to Jesus to save souls, poor souls! They have less grace than we have, and still all the blood of a God was shed to save them.

And yet Jesus wills to make their salvation depend on one sigh from our heart. [In other words, Thérèse must intercede and offer her sufferings for the conversion of sinners.]

What a mystery! If one sigh can save a soul, what can sufferings like ours not do? Let us refuse Jesus nothing! (GC I 546–47)

Peace in Suffering

Let us see life as it really is. It is a moment between two eternities. Let us suffer in peace! I admit that this word "peace" seemed a little strong to me, but the other day, when reflecting on it, I found the secret of suffering in peace. The one who says *peace* is not saying joy, or at least, felt joy. To suffer in peace it is enough to will all that Jesus wills. (GC I 553)

When we are suffering, it does so much good to have friendly hearts whose echo responds to our own sorrow! (GC I 555)

Joy isn't found in the objects that surround us; it's found in the innermost recesses of the soul. One can possess it as well in a prison as in a palace. (SS Edmonson 156)

Prudent and Never Despairing

In spite of her love for suffering, Thérèse was prudent about how she prayed for it. She was careful not to go beyond what God himself had for her.

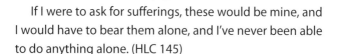

If I were to ask for sufferings, these would be mine, and I would have to bear them alone, and I've never been able to do anything alone. (HLC 145)

Thérèse never allowed her suffering to take the form of melancholy or of depression over her short-comings. When Pauline confided that she felt sad and discouraged over her faults, Thérèse responded in her practical, upbeat way.

You don't act like me. When I commit a fault that makes me sad, I know very well that the sadness is a consequence of my infidelity, but do you believe I remain there? Oh! No, I'm not so foolish! I hasten to say to God: My God, I know I have merited this feeling of sadness, but let me offer it up to you just the same as a trial that you sent me through love. I'm sorry for my sin, but I'm happy to have this suffering to offer to you. (HLC 71)

We who run in the way of love shouldn't be thinking of sufferings that can take place in the future; it's a lack of confidence, it's like meddling in the work of creation. (HLC 106)

Reflection

Many Christians today claim that God automatically blesses believers with prosperity and freedom from pain. Thérèse would vigorously refute this, pointing to the example of Jesus himself.

Not all suffering should be endured, of course. Emotional and physical pain that can be eased should be eased. Beyond that, however, life is full of difficulty. We can ignore it or avoid it, or we can profit from it. As St. Francis of Assisi said when speaking of suffering, this was God's life on earth, so what choice do we have but to make it our own?

Prayer

Lord, help me to accept the suffering that comes my way. I want to overcome my fear, and, through my pain, I want to draw closer to you. In the dark night of my suffering, you alone are my light. Through Christ our Lord, Amen.

Chapter Four

THE LITTLE WAY

Years ago, Mother Teresa of Calcutta established a house for her Missionaries of Charity in a run-down neighborhood in Washington, DC. The press was on hand when she arrived to help her sisters settle in, and one reporter asked what she hoped to accomplish there.

"The joy of loving and being loved," she replied.

The reporter pointed out that, in these circumstances, that would take a lot of money. Mother Teresa corrected him. No, she said, it would take a lot of sacrifice.

One hundred years earlier, Thérèse of Lisieux hit upon the same answer to many of life's problems: sacrifice. Money and social position were not the answer, Thérèse decided, but countless small sacrifices offered to God might count for much.

This sort of hidden, quiet life didn't automatically appeal to Thérèse. Actually, she longed for a heroic life in which she could die as a martyr or spend herself as a missionary. But she lacked the stamina and opportunity for a rigorous, public ministry, and so she sought a more realistic path to God.

This turned out to be her Little Way of spiritual childhood, characterized by humility and childlike confidence in God. Thérèse concluded that God himself would lift her to the heights of sanctity if she would rely on him as a child relies on her parents.

Personal need drove Thérèse to develop her approach, but it's a method available to anyone, anytime, anywhere and requires only the will to serve God and others in small, everyday ways.

This Little Way often found expression in small sacrifices and acts of kindness done in secret. When doing the laundry in the heat of summer, for example, Thérèse chose the hottest place in the room, leaving the cooler places to the other nuns. Thérèse suffered intensely from the frigid winter weather in the unheated convent. She never complained, however, and only on her deathbed did she reveal that during some of the winters, she thought she would die of the cold.

Thérèse's Little Way couldn't be more easy to adopt. It encompasses all the virtues, such as humility, love of neighbor, and trust in God, but it doesn't require a complicated scheme to carry it off. All that's necessary is the desire to put God and others first and ourselves second.

The Little Way was Thérèse's response to the invasion of her heart by Jesus. His love for her overwhelmed her. She, in turn, wanted to love him passionately, to heap upon him every sign of her love for as long as she had the strength to do so. She did this dozens of times a day through the most mundane sacrifices and kindnesses.

It worked. Her life was hidden and her sacrifices were small, but they earned her a place in heaven and the honor of the church.

Smallness Before the Lord

Thérèse felt that she didn't have what it takes to be a saint. She was too inconsequential—too small—to achieve great sanctity. One day, the Lord revealed to her that he honored her littleness and, in fact, wanted her to remain that way. He himself would provide the way for Thérèse—and all those who have a simple trust in him—to reach heaven.

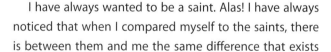

I have always wanted to be a saint. Alas! I have always noticed that when I compared myself to the saints, there is between them and me the same difference that exists between a mountain whose summit is lost in the clouds and the obscure grain of sand trampled underfoot by the passers-by.

Instead of becoming discouraged, I said to myself: God cannot inspire unrealizable desires. I can, then, in spite of my littleness, aspire to holiness. . . . I want to seek out a means of going to heaven by a little way, a way that is very straight, very short, and totally new.

We are living now in an age of inventions, and we no longer have to take the trouble of climbing stairs, for, in the homes of the rich, an elevator has replaced these very successfully. I wanted to find an elevator which would raise me to Jesus, for I am too small to climb the rough stairway of perfection.

I searched, then, in the Scriptures for some sign of this elevator, the object of my desires, and I read these words coming from the mouth of eternal wisdom: "Whoever is a little one, let him come to me [Proverbs 9:4]." And so I succeeded. I felt I had found what I was looking for. But wanting to know, O my God, what you would do to the very little one who answered your call, I continued my search and this is what I discovered: "As one whom a mother caresses, so will I comfort you; you shall be carried at the breasts, and upon the knees they shall caress you" [Isaiah 66:13, 12].

The elevator which must raise me to heaven is your arms, O Jesus. (SS Clarke 207–8)

My way is all confidence and love. I do not understand souls who fear a friend so tender. At times, when I am reading certain spiritual treatises in which perfection is shown through a thousand obstacles, surrounded by a crowd of illusions, my poor little mind quickly tires; I close the learned book that is breaking my head and drying up my heart, and I take up holy Scripture.

Then all seems luminous to me; a single word uncovers for my soul infinite horizons, perfection seems simple to me, I see it is sufficient to recognize one's nothingness and to abandon oneself as a child into God's arms. Leaving to great souls, to great minds the beautiful books I cannot understand, much less put into practice, I rejoice at being little since children alone and those who resemble them will be admitted to the heavenly banquet. (GC II 1094)

Speaking of herself as a child of the church, Thérèse wrote,

———————⧓———————

The child understands that glory belongs by right to her brothers and sisters, the angels and the saints. . . . What she asks for is love; she knows only one thing, and that is to love you, Jesus.

Dazzling works are forbidden to her; she cannot preach the gospel or shed her blood. But what does it matter? Her brothers and sisters are working in place of her, and she, the little child, remains very close to the throne of the king and queen, and she loves in the place of her brothers and sisters who are going into combat.

But how will she bear witness to her love, since love is proved by works? Well, the little child will throw out flowers, she will use her perfumes to give a lovely fragrance to the royal throne, she will sing with her silvery voice the hymn of love.

Yes, my Beloved, that is how my life will be consumed. I have no other means of proving my love for you than to throw flowers, that is, not to pass up any little sacrifice, any look, any word, to take advantage of all the little things and to do them out of love. (SS Edmonson 219–20)

A Hidden Life of Sacrifice

With astonishing confidence, Thérèse declared on several occasions that she would be a saint. She would achieve that distinction through her hidden, silent life of sacrifice.

———— ⬿ ————

God let me feel that true glory is the one that will last forever, and that to obtain it, it isn't necessary to do outstanding works, but to remain hidden and to practice virtue in such a way that the right hand doesn't know what the left hand is doing [Matthew 6:3].

So, when I was reading the tales of the patriotic actions of French heroines, in particular those of the Venerable Joan of Arc, I had a great desire to imitate them. It seemed to me that I felt within me the same burning desire that stirred them, the same heavenly inspiration.

Then I received a grace that I have always regarded as one of the greatest of my life. . . . I thought that I was born for glory, . . . that my own glory wouldn't be apparent to mortal eyes, that it would consist in becoming a great saint!

This desire might seem foolhardy if one were to consider how weak and imperfect I was, and how much I still am after seven years spent in the religious life, but nonetheless I still feel the same audacious confidence that I'll become a great saint.

That's because I'm not counting on my merits, since I have none, but I hope in the one who is virtue, holiness itself. It is he alone who, being content with my feeble efforts, will raise me up to himself and, covering me with his infinite merits, will make me a saint. I wasn't thinking then that one has to suffer a great deal to arrive at sainthood, but God wasn't long in showing me this. (SS Edmonson 70–71)

Thérèse had hoped to enter Carmel before Lent of 1888. For various reasons, however, she was denied admission until after Easter. She was tempted to relax her strict preparations for the convent but decided, instead, to continue her mortifications. True to her Little Way, these penances were very simple and ordinary.

How did these three months go by, these months that were so rich in graces for my soul? At first the thought came to me of not bothering to live as strict a life as I was used to doing. But soon I understood the value of the time that was being offered to me, and I resolved to give myself over more than ever to a serious and mortified life.

When I say mortified, this is not to make you believe that I was always doing penances. Alas! I never did a single one. Far from being like those beautiful souls who from childhood practiced every kind of mortifications, I felt no attraction for them. . . .

Instead of that I let myself always be coddled in cotton and fattened up like a little bird that has no need of doing penance.

My mortifications consisted in breaking my will, which was always ready to impose itself; in holding my tongue instead of answering back; in doing little things for others without hoping to get anything in return; in not slumping back when I was sitting down, etc., etc.

It was through the practice of these little nothings that I prepared myself to become Jesus' bride. (SS Edmonson 164–65)

The War Against Herself

Thérèse had neither the opportunity nor, as she matured, the inclination to perform rigorous penances. Her life in the convent was extremely ascetical, but beyond that she viewed penance from the perspective of her Little Way. In the next excerpts, she comments on the penitential practices of the saints.

Our Lord assured us . . . that in his Father's house there are many mansions. If every soul called to perfection were obliged to perform these austerities in order to enter heaven, our Lord would have given us some clear indication of it and we would respond eagerly. But he himself has declared, "In my Father's house there are many mansions" [John 14:2].

If, then, there are mansions set apart for great souls, for the fathers of the desert and for the martyrs of penance, there must also be one for little children. So a place is waiting for us there if we but love him dearly together with our heavenly Father and the Spirit of Love. (MSST 48)

A passage in the life of Blessed Henry Suso struck me with regard to corporal penances. He had performed frightful penances which had destroyed his health; an angel appeared to him, telling him to stop. Then he added: "You are no longer to fight as a simple soldier; from this moment I shall arm you as a knight." And he made the saint understand the superiority of the spiritual combat over corporal mortifications.

Well . . . God didn't want me to be a simple soldier; I was armed from the beginning as a knight, and I went out to war against self in the spiritual domain, through self-denial in hidden sacrifices.

I discovered peace and humility in this obscure struggle in which nature finds nothing for self. (HLC 130)

I applied myself above all to practicing the little virtues, since I didn't have the facility for practicing the big ones. So I loved to fold the mantles that had been forgotten by the sisters, and to do all the little services for them that I could. . . .

My fervor would no doubt not have lasted long if I had been assigned many penances to do. The ones that were given to me without my asking for them consisted in mortifying my self-love, which did me much more good than bodily penances. (SS Edmonson 181–82)

Small Sacrifices and the Virtue of Detachment

Its not easy to act on the small sacrificial opportunities that come our way every day. Thérèse offers a suggestion for overcoming our reluctance.

Many souls say: I don't have the strength to accomplish this sacrifice. Let them do, then, what I did: exert a great effort. God never refuses that first grace that gives one the courage to act; afterwards, the heart is strengthened and one advances from victory to victory. (HLC 142)

Thérèse's Little Way includes the virtue of detachment. When helping with the formation of the novices, she practiced this virtue not only for its own sake but also with an eye to her goal of serving her sisters.

When I am talking with a novice, I try to mortify myself as I do so. I avoid asking her questions that would satisfy my curiosity. If she begins an interesting topic and then passes on to another that annoys me without finishing the first one, I take care not to remind her about the subject she has left aside, because it seems to me that you can't do any good when you're seeking yourself. (SS Edmonson 288)

Here, Thérèse gives a fellow nun advice on how she ought to approach her work.

Keep yourself interiorly detached and free from any piece of work you might be doing. Always let the nuns give you advice and suggestions about it and do not object if they touch it up, even in your absence.

Naturally, because of differences of taste, they might, in this way, spoil it and you will begin to count as wasted the hours you have devoted to it. . . .

The goal of all our undertakings should not be so much a task perfectly completed but the accomplishment of the will of God. (MSST 173)

When I am feeling nothing, when I am incapable of praying, of practicing virtue, then is the moment for seeking opportunities, nothings, which please Jesus more than mastery of the world or even martyrdom suffered with generosity. For example, a smile, a friendly word, when I would want to say nothing, or put on a look of annoyance. (GC II 801)

Love is nourished only by sacrifices, and the more a soul refuses natural satisfactions, the stronger and more disinterested becomes her tenderness. (SS Clarke 237)

It is the little crosses that are our whole joy; they are more common than big ones and prepare the heart to receive the latter when this is the will of our good Master. (GC II 816)

Reflection

For Thérèse, entering the convent was something like entering the spiritual equivalent of the Olympics. The nuns weren't in competition with each other, of course, but their training pushed them to achieve their personal best. They learned to endure suffering and practice self-denial in the pursuit of their goal.

Flannery O'Connor once said, "It is the extreme situation that best reveals what we are essentially."[1] Thérèse was essentially a lover of God and his people. Her Little Way pushed her into the extremes of sacrifice, and there her holiness was revealed.

Prayer

Lord, opportunities for holiness are all around me. Every day I miss many chances to serve others in "little ways" and to offer small sacrifices to you. Help me seize the moment, confident that you will give me the grace to triumph over my own laziness and reluctance to serve. Through Christ our Lord, Amen.

1. Flannery O'Connor, *Mystery and Manners*, Sally and Robert Fitzgerald, ed. (New York: Farrar, Strauss & Giroux, 1969), 113.

Chapter Five

HUMILITY: NOTHING TO GIVE BUT GIVING IT ALL

Most of Thérèse's fellow nuns regarded her as a good nun, even an exceptional nun, but nothing more—certainly not a saint. Her sister Céline summed up the general feeling when she said that no one ever noticed anything particularly unusual or extraordinary about Thérèse.

There is a famous story about Thérèse and the obituary notice that Carmelite convents customarily sent to one another on the death of one of their own. One of the sisters was speculating on what the mother prioress could possibly find to say about Thérèse. Of course, she is very good, the sister said dismissively, but she's never done anything worth talking about.

Nothing could have pleased Thérèse more, except not to have been noticed at all. She wanted to be trampled underfoot like a grain of sand, she said, to be forgotten, not only by the rest of the world but also by herself.

Thérèse wasn't suffering from a massive case of low self-esteem, as these statements might indicate. On the contrary, she had an extremely healthy ego.

God had created her and he had redeemed her. Not for a moment did she doubt her self-worth.

The point of Thérèse's humility was simply to clear the ground so that Jesus alone could live within her. This "littleness" allowed her to see herself as she really was—imperfect and dependent on God—but freed her from an excessive preoccupation with her own short-comings. She urged others to simply love Jesus without spending a lot of time scrutinizing their faults.

Thérèse never gave in to false modesty or self-pity, two traits commonly mistaken for humility. Nor was she passive. She may have been weak and little, as she said, but she wasn't helpless. She pursued humility with an almost frightening intensity. It was, in fact, the basis for her Little Way.

The glory of Jesus, she said, is what it's all about. By vigorously emptying herself for him, she hoped to imitate and attract him who had emptied himself for her.

Humbleness of Heart

Let us never speak [of] what appears great in the eyes of creatures. Solomon, the wisest king who ever was on earth, having considered the different works that occupy men under the sun, painting, sculpture, all the arts, understood that all these things were subject to envy; he cried out that they were only vanity and affliction of spirit [Wisdom 1:14]!

The only thing that is not envied is the last place; there is, then, only this last place which is not vanity and affliction of spirit. (GC II 1121)

How little known are the goodness, the merciful love of Jesus. . . . It is true, to enjoy these treasures one must humble oneself, recognizing one's nothingness, and that is what many souls do not want to do. (GC II 1165)

In a letter to Céline, Thérèse urges her sister to remain humble and faithful to God in small things:

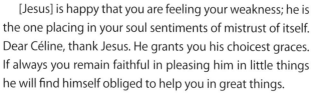

[Jesus] is happy that you are feeling your weakness; he is the one placing in your soul sentiments of mistrust of itself. Dear Céline, thank Jesus. He grants you his choicest graces. If always you remain faithful in pleasing him in little things he will find himself obliged to help you in great things.

The apostles worked all night without our Lord and they caught no fish, but their work was pleasing to Jesus. He willed to prove to them that he alone can give us something; he willed that the apostles humble themselves. "Children," he said to them, "have you nothing to eat?" "Lord," St. Peter answered, "we have fished all night and have caught nothing" [John 21:4-5]. Perhaps if he had caught some little fish, Jesus would not have performed the miracle, but he had nothing, so Jesus soon filled his net in such a way as almost to break it.

This is the character of Jesus: he gives as God, but he wills humility of heart. (GC II 851)

Whenever you are lacking in virtue, you should not excuse yourself by throwing the blame on physical causes, on the weather, or some other trial. Instead, you should make it a means of self-humiliation and then go to take your place in the rank and file of little souls, since you are so weak in the practice of virtue.

Your soul's urgent need at present is not the ability to practice heroic virtue, but rather to acquire humility. (MSST 24)

Alas! When I think of the time of my novitiate I see how imperfect I was. I made so much fuss over such little things that it makes me laugh now. . . . Later on, no doubt, the time in which I am now will appear filled with imperfections, but now I am astonished at nothing. I am not disturbed at seeing myself weakness itself.

On the contrary, it is in my weakness that I glory [2 Corinthians 12:5], and I expect each day to discover new imperfections in myself. (SS Clarke 224)

Devotion to the Holy Face

Thérèse's full name as a religious was Thérèse of the Child Jesus and the Holy Face. "The Holy Face" is a reference to the face of Jesus disfigured by suffering as described in Isaiah 52. The total humility depicted there motivated her spiritual life.

———————

These words of Isaiah: "Who has believed our report? . . . There is no beauty in him, no comeliness, etc." [Isaiah 53:1-2], have made the whole foundation of my devotion to the Holy Face, or, to express it better, the foundation of all my piety. I, too, have desired to be without beauty, alone in treading the winepress, unknown to everyone. (HLC 135)

Pauline first introduced Thérèse to the devotion of the Holy Face. Here she reminds Pauline of that and reveals the impact this devotion has had on her spirituality.

———————

I had never fathomed the depths of the treasures hidden in the Holy Face. It was through you . . . that I learned to know these treasures. Just as . . . you had preceded us into Carmel, so also you were first to enter deeply into the mysteries of love hidden in the face of our Spouse. You called me and I understood. I understood what real glory was.

He whose kingdom is not of this world [John 18:36] showed me that true wisdom consists in "desiring to be unknown and counted as nothing," in "placing one's joy in the contempt of self."

Ah! I desired that, like the face of Jesus, "my face be truly hidden, that no one on earth would know me" [Isaiah 53:3]. (SS Clarke 152)

True Nobility

Louis Martin, Thérèse, and Céline went on a pilgrimage to Rome shortly before Thérèse entered Carmel. The wealth and social position of the others on the trip prompted Thérèse to reflect on true nobility.

Céline and I found ourselves in the midst of the nobility who almost exclusively made up the pilgrimage. Ah! Far from dazzling us, all these titles and these "de" appeared to us as nothing but smoke. . . . I understood the words of *The Imitation [of Christ]*: "Be not solicitous for the shadow of a great name!" . . .

I understood true greatness is to be found in the soul, not in a name, since as Isaiah says: "The Lord will call his servants by another name" [Isaiah 65:15], and St. John says: "To him that overcomes I will give a white stone, and on the stone a new name written which no man knows but the one who receives it" [Revelation 2:17].

It is in heaven, then, that we shall know our titles of nobility. Then shall every man have praise from God [1 Corinthians 4:5] and the one who on earth wanted to be the poorest, the most forgotten out of love of Jesus, will be the first, the noblest, and the richest! (SS Clarke 121–22)

At the beginning of my spiritual life when I was thirteen or fourteen, I used to ask myself what I would have to strive for later on because I believed it was quite impossible for me to understand perfection better.

I learned very quickly since then that the more one advances, the more one sees the goal is still far off. And now I am simply resigned to see myself always imperfect and in this I find joy. (SS Clarke 158)

We should . . . attribute nothing of good to ourselves. No one actually possesses the virtues he practices, so let everything redound to the glory of God.

God has need of no one, so let us not take foolish pride in the thought that he decides to make use of us at times. (MSST 205)

A Share in Jesus' Humiliation

On her pilgrimage to Rome, Thérèse noticed that there were greater restrictions placed on women than on men. Women, for example, were not allowed in certain parts of shrines or churches. She saw this as an opportunity to share in Jesus' humiliation but left the matter open, to be settled in heaven.

Poor women, how they are disparaged! However, they love God in much greater numbers than men, and during the passion of our Lord, the women had more courage than the apostles [Luke 23: 27] since they braved the insults of the soldiers and dared to wipe the adorable face of Jesus.

It's no doubt for that reason that he allows scorn to be their lot on earth, since he chose that for himself. In heaven he'll know how to show that his thoughts are not man's thoughts [Isaiah 55:8-9], because then the last will be the first [Matthew 20:16]. (SS Edmonson 159)

My life has been a happy one because I have tried to put self-seeking away from me. The only way to attain happiness is to know perfect love. And the only way to attain perfect love is to forget self entirely and never to seek gratification in anything. (MSST 144)

Those who judge you unfavorably are not robbing you of anything; you are none the poorer for all they may say. It is they who are really the losers. . . . Is there anything sweeter than the inward joy that comes from thinking well of others!

If, for the love of God, you truly humble yourself when judged unfavorably by others, it is all the better for you and all the worse for your critics. (MSST 28)

Thérèse stressed the importance of relying on God's strength, not our own. Had St. Peter done so, he would never have endured the humiliation of denying Jesus before the crucifixion.

Look at little children: they never stop breaking things, tearing things, falling down, and they do this even while loving their parents very, very much. When I fall in this way, it makes me realize my nothingness more, and I say to myself: What would I do, and what would I become, if I were I to rely on my own strength?

I understand very well why St. Peter fell. Poor Peter, he was relying upon himself instead of relying only upon God's strength. . . . I'm very sure that if St. Peter had said humbly to Jesus: "Give me the grace, I beg you, to follow you even to death," he would have received it immediately.

I'm very certain that our Lord didn't say anymore to his apostles through his instructions and his physical presence than he says to us through his good inspirations and his grace. He could have said to Peter: "Ask me for the strength to accomplish what you want." But no, he didn't, because he wanted to show him his weakness, and because, before ruling the church that is filled with sinners, he had to experience for himself what man is able to do without God's help.

And before Peter fell, our Lord had said to him: "And once you are converted, strengthen your brethren." This means: Convince them of the weakness of human strength through your own experience. (HLC 140)

Better Not to Fight

Thérèse's humility was such that she would admit she was not always able to respond to a difficult situation with love. When that was the case, she simply fled. Here, she gives an example not only of this stratagem but of her own imperfection and humble willingness to see herself as she was. She is speaking to her mother superior.

I have already told you that my last means of not being defeated in combats is desertion; I was already using this means during my novitiate, and it always succeeded perfectly with me. I wish, Mother, to give you an example which I believe will make you smile.

During one of your bronchial attacks, I came to your cell very quietly one morning to return the keys of the Communion grating since I was sacristan. I wasn't too displeased at having this opportunity to see you; I was very much pleased but I didn't dare to show it.

A sister, animated with holy zeal . . . believed I was going to awaken you when she saw me entering your quarters; she wanted to take the keys away from me. I was too stubborn to give them to her and to cede my rights. As politely as I could, I told her that it was my duty to return the keys.

I understand now that it would have been more perfect to cede to this sister. . . . I did not understand it at the time, and as I wanted absolutely to enter in spite of the fact that she was pushing the door to prevent me, very soon the thing we feared most happened: the racket we were making made you open your eyes. Then, Mother, everything tumbled upon me. The poor sister I had resisted began to deliver a whole discourse, the gist of which was: "It's Sister Thérèse of the Child Jesus who made the noise; my God, how disagreeable she is, etc."

I, who felt just the contrary, had a great desire to defend myself. Happily, there came a bright idea into my mind, and I told myself that if I began to justify myself I would not be able to retain my peace of soul. I felt, too, that I did not have enough virtue to permit myself to be accused without saying a word. My last plank of salvation was in flight. No sooner thought than done. I left without fuss, allowing the sister to continue her discourse which resembled the imprecations of Camillus against the city of Rome. My heart was beating so rapidly that it was impossible for me to go far. . . . There was no bravery there, Mother; however, I believe it was much better for me not to expose myself to combat when there was certain defeat facing me. (SS Clarke 223–24)

Opportunities to Grow in Humility

Although she was never officially appointed to the office, Thérèse served as the mistress of novices. The novices heaped praise on her, which distressed Thérèse. Since she always allowed them to speak freely to her, however, occasionally one of them would criticize her severely. Thérèse accepted such reprimands as an opportunity to grow in humility.

Sometimes there comes to me a great desire to hear something else besides praises. . . . Jesus permits someone to serve [my soul] a good little salad, well seasoned with vinegar and spices, nothing is missing except the oil which gives it added flavor.

This good little salad is served up to me by the novices at a time when I least expect it. God lifts the veil which hides my imperfections, and then my dear little sisters, seeing me just as I am, no longer find me according to their taste.

With a simplicity which delights me, they tell me all the struggles I give them, what displeases them in me; finally they are under no restraint any more than if they were talking about another person, for they know they give me pleasure when acting in this way. . . .

One day when I particularly desired to be humiliated, a novice took it upon herself to satisfy me and she did it so well that I was immediately reminded of Semei cursing David [2 Samuel 16:10]. I said to myself: Yes, it is the Lord who has commanded her to say all these things to me. And my soul enjoyed the bitter food served up to it in such abundance.

This is the way God sees fit to take care of me. He cannot always be giving me the strengthening bread of exterior humiliation, but from time to time he allows me to be fed the crumbs which fall from the table of his children [Mark 7:28]. (SS Clarke 244–45)

Jesus, Our Model of Humility

Jesus himself was the model for Thérèse's humility. He leaves himself vulnerable to us, in a manner of speaking, waiting for but never demanding our love.

131

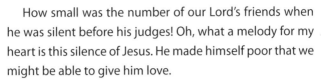

How small was the number of our Lord's friends when he was silent before his judges! Oh, what a melody for my heart is this silence of Jesus. He made himself poor that we might be able to give him love.

He holds out his hand to us like a beggar so that on the radiant day of judgment when he will appear in his glory, he may have us hear those sweet words: "Come, blessed of my Father, for I was hungry and you gave me to eat; I was thirsty, and you gave me to drink; I did not know where to lodge, and you gave me a home. I was in prison, sick, and you helped me" [Matthew 25:34-36].

It is Jesus himself who spoke these words; it is he who wants our love, who begs for it. He places himself, so to speak, at our mercy, he does not want to take anything unless we give it to him, and the smallest thing is precious in his divine eyes. . . .

We must be like Jesus, Jesus whose face was hidden. [Isaiah 53:3]. "Do you want to learn something that may be of use to you?" says *The Imitation [of Christ]*. "Love to be unknown and accounted for nothing." And elsewhere: "After you have left everything, you must above all leave yourself." (GC II 808–9)

In a letter to her cousin, Marie Guérin, Thérèse reveals more of her understanding of humility:

If you are nothing, you must not forget that Jesus is all, so you must lose your little nothingness in his infinite all and think only of this uniquely lovable all.

Neither ought you desire to see the fruit gathered from your efforts, for Jesus is pleased to keep for himself alone these little nothings that console him.

You are mistaken, my darling, if you believe that your little Thérèse walks always with fervor on the road of virtue. She is weak and very weak, and everyday she has a new experience of this weakness but, Marie, Jesus is pleased to teach her, as he did St. Paul, the science of rejoicing in her infirmities [2 Corinthians 12:5].

This is a great grace, and I beg Jesus to teach it to you, for peace and quiet of heart are to be found there only. (GC I 641)

As a Grain of Sand

The things of the world had no interest for Thérèse. She understood God's love so completely that she wanted nothing to stand in the way of receiving him. Here she speaks of herself in the third person, as a grain of sand.

How it [the grain of sand] longs to be reduced to nothing, to be unknown by all creatures. . . . Poor little thing, it desires nothing any longer, nothing but to be forgotten . . . not contempt, insults, this would be too glorious for a grain of sand.

Yes, I want to be forgotten, and this, not only by creatures but by myself. I'd like to be reduced to nothing to such an extent as to have no desire whatsoever.

The glory of Jesus, that is all; as for my own glory, I abandon it to him, and, if he seems to forget me, he is free since I am no longer my own but his. And he will more quickly grow tired of making me wait than I shall grow tired of waiting for him! (GC I 612)

Intellect Subject to Humility

A person possessing intellectual gifts and spiritual insights can easily succumb to arrogance. Blessed with abundant wisdom, Thérèse herself found it difficult to avoid a sense of pride in her ability. Eventually, she realized that the intellect is as subject to humility as any other aspect of the personality.

The good things that come directly from God—upward risings of the mind and the heart, deep thoughts—all those things form riches to which one can become attached as much as to a material thing that no one has the right to touch.

For example, if during a break someone says to a sister some revelation received during the time of prayer, and then, a short time later, when speaking to another sister, that sister says the thing that had been confided in her as if she had thought of it herself, it seems as if she's taking something that isn't hers.

Or if during a recreation period, someone says quietly to her neighbor an appropriate word that's full of spirit, and the second sister repeats the word out loud without letting others know the source from which it comes, again, that seems to be stealing from the owner, who doesn't claim it but would really like to do so and seize on the first opportunity to delicately let it be known that someone has grabbed one of her thoughts. . . .

I wouldn't be able to explain . . . so well these sad reactions of nature, if I hadn't felt them in my heart . . . [but] now I can say it: Jesus has given me the grace not to be more attached to the things of the mind and the heart than to those of earth.

If it happens to me to think and to say something that pleases my sisters, I find it quite natural for them to take it over as belonging to themselves. That thought belongs to the Holy Spirit and not to me, since St. Paul said that without the Spirit of Love we can't give the name "Father" to our Father who is in heaven [Romans 8:15]. So he's quite free to use me to give a good thought to a soul.

If I believed that thought belongs to me, I would be like the "donkey bearing relics" who thought that the homage being paid to the saints was addressed to him. (SS Edmonson 262–63)

Reflection

St. John Vianney, the Curé of Ars, had tremendous spiritual insights and spectacular success in bringing people to the Lord. Of his extraordinary ministry he simply said that he had been privileged to give great gifts from his empty hands.

In his unassuming way, the Curé captured much of Thérèse's thinking on humility. Both would agree on the importance of this virtue. Both practiced it so intensely that it produced great sanctity. Thérèse urged all those interested in holiness to embrace it.

Certainly it is one of the most appealing, if least practiced, virtues. If we make it ours, we too will find that the Lord will give the greatest gift—himself—through our empty hands.

Prayer

How humble you were, Lord, to come to earth in the form of a man. Free me from the pride that prevents me from imitating your humility. Help me to see that the greatest person is the one who quietly serves the needs of others. Through Christ our Lord, Amen.

Chapter Six

DIFFICULTIES IN PRAYER

At the minimum, most of us expect saints to stay awake when they pray. Of course, we expect much more than that—revelations and ecstasies, for example—but at the very least we assume that they'll remain alert. In a striking departure from tradition, Thérèse slept—not always but often enough.

Although she loved prayer, she grew distracted, found group prayer difficult, and experienced tremendous spiritual aridity. Her sister Céline said that she didn't think a soul ever received less consolation in prayer than Thérèse.

At last, a saint most people can identify with! True to her Little Way, Thérèse once said that she wanted there to be nothing about her that other people might envy. This extended to her prayer life. The more ordinary that was, the more readily people could identify with it.

During her seven years in the convent, Thérèse did receive occasional consolations in prayer, but these were extremely rare and virtually ceased toward the end. Mystical moments of prayer were not the rule for Thérèse, her sister Pauline said. Simplicity was.

Thérèse herself said she could think of no ecstasy that would appeal to her more than sacrifice. She found her happiness in sacrificial self-offering alone.

In spite of the difficulties, Thérèse remained faithful to prayer and relished her time with the Lord. She was there to love and comfort him, demanding no comfort in return. The fact that she received none is meant to encourage rather than discourage us.

Her prayer life underlines the point that holiness doesn't rest on warm feelings, visions, and prophecies but on the attitude of the heart before God.

Spiritual Dryness in Prayer

In her autobiography, Thérèse explains how she handled the spiritual dryness that plagued her. She focuses on the retreat she attended before taking her vows as a Carmelite.

———————

[The retreat] was far from bringing me any consolations since the most absolute aridity and almost total abandonment were my lot.

Jesus was sleeping as usual in my little boat. . . . I see very well how rarely souls allow him to sleep peacefully within them. Jesus is so fatigued with always having to take the initiative and attend to others that he hastens to take advantage of the repose I offer him. . . .

Really, I am far from being a saint, and what I have just said is proof of this; instead of rejoicing, for example, at my aridity, I should attribute it to my little fervor and lack of fidelity; I should be desolate for having slept (for seven years) during my hours of prayer and my thanksgivings after holy Communion; well, I am not desolate.

I remember that little children are as pleasing to their parents when they are asleep as well as when they are wide awake; I remember, too, that when they perform operations, doctors put their patients to sleep. Finally, I remember that: "The Lord knows our weakness, that he is mindful that we are but dust and ashes" [Psalm 102:14]. (SS Clarke 165)

I can't say that I frequently received consolations when making my thanksgivings after Mass; perhaps it is the time when I receive the least. However, I find this very understandable since I have offered myself to Jesus not as one desirous of her own consolation in his visit but simply to please him who is giving himself to me.

When I am preparing for holy Communion, I picture my soul as a piece of land and I beg the Blessed Virgin to remove from it any rubbish that would prevent it from being free; then I ask her to set up a huge tent worthy of heaven, adorning it with her own jewelry; finally, I invite all the angels and saints to come and conduct a magnificent concert there. It seems to me that when Jesus descends into my heart he is content to find himself so well received and I, too, am content.

All this, however, does not prevent both distractions and sleepiness from visiting me, but at the end of the thanksgiving when I see that I've made it so badly I make a resolution to be thankful all through the rest of the day. (SS Clarke 172–73)

One scientist said, "Give me a lever, a point to support it, and I will lift the world." What Archimedes was unable to obtain because his request wasn't made to God and was made only from a material point of view, the saints obtained in all its fullness. The Almighty gave them, as a point of support, himself, and himself alone. As a lever: prayer, which sets ablaze a fire of love, and that's how they lifted the world. That's how all the saints who are still fighting the battle lift it, and that's how until the end of the world the saints to come will lift it as well. (SS Edmonson 296)

It's prayer, it's sacrifice that are entirely my strength. These are the invincible weapons that Jesus has given me. Much more than words, they can touch souls. (SS Edmonson 272)

The recitation of the rosary costs me more than one instrument of penance, I feel that I say it so poorly. It's in vain that I attempt to meditate on the mysteries of the rosary—I don't succeed in engaging my mind.

For a long time I was extremely sorry for this lack of devotion that surprised me, because I love the Blessed Virgin so much that it ought to be easy for me to pray in her honor prayers that are pleasing to her.

Now I'm less sorry, because I think that since the Queen of Heaven is my mother, she must see my good will and is happy with it.

Sometimes when my mind is in such dryness that it's impossible for me to pull a thought out of it to unite myself to God, I very slowly recite an Our Father and a Hail Mary. Then those prayers delight me; they nourish my soul more than if I had recited them hurriedly a hundred times.

The Blessed Virgin shows me that she's not angry with me; she never fails to protect me as soon as I invoke her. If some sort of worry, some difficulty, overtakes me, quickly I turn toward her and always, like the most tender of mothers, she shoulders my interest. (SS Edmonson 274–75)

How many lights have I not drawn from the works of . . . St. John of the Cross! At the ages of seventeen and eighteen I had no other spiritual nourishment; later on, however, all books left me in aridity and I'm still in that state.

If I open a book composed by a spiritual author (even the most beautiful, the most touching book), I feel my heart contract immediately and I read without understanding, so to speak. Or if I do understand, my mind comes to a standstill without the capacity of meditating. In this helplessness, holy Scripture and *The Imitation [of Christ]* come to my aid; in them I discover a solid and very pure nourishment.

But it is especially the gospels which sustain me during my hours of prayer, for in them I find what is necessary for my poor little soul. I am constantly discovering in them new lights, hidden and mysterious meanings.

I understand and I know from experience that: "The kingdom of God is within you" [Luke 17:21]. . . . Never have I heard [Jesus] speak, but I feel that he is within me at each moment; he is guiding and inspiring me with what I must say and do.

I find just when I need them certain lights which I had not seen until then, and it isn't most frequently during my hours of prayer that these are most abundant but rather in the midst of my daily occupations. (SS Clarke 179)

The Power of Prayer

Although Thérèse didn't think she was capable of composing lengthy, beautiful prayers, she was confident that God would hear and respond to her simple entreaties.

How great is the power of prayer. It's like a queen's having constant free access to the king and being able to obtain all that she asks. It's not necessary in order for a prayer to be granted to read in a book a beautiful formula composed for the circumstances. If that were the case, alas! How I should be pitied!

Outside of the Divine Office . . . which I'm very unworthy to recite, I don't have the courage to make a strict rule for myself to search in books for beautiful prayers. That gives me a headache, there are so many of them! And then some are more beautiful than others, I wouldn't know how to recite them all.

Not knowing which one to choose, I do as children do who don't know how to read: I very simply tell God what I want to tell him without making beautiful phrases, and he always understands me.

For me, prayer is an upward rising of the heart, it's a simple glance toward heaven, it's a cry of gratitude and love in the midst of trials as much as in the midst of joys. In short, it's something big, something great, something supernatural, that expands my heart and unites me to Jesus. (SS Edmonson 273–75)

Reflection

There is a popular story from the life of St. John Vianney, the Curé of Ars, regarding a peasant from his parish. The peasant sat in church for a long time every day, and Vianney asked him what he did as he sat there. "I look at him," the man answered, "and he looks at me, and we are happy together."

Thérèse would have approved of this man's simple, heartfelt approach to prayer. We may find prayer challenging, as she did, or serene, as the peasant did. The important thing is simply that we do pray, recognizing that prayer is not an end in itself but the opportunity for a personal encounter with God.

Prayer

Help me to be like Thérèse, Lord: faithful to prayer even when I'm tired or bored or feel that you don't hear me. As I reach out to you, reach out to me and draw me near through our mutual conversation. Through Christ our Lord, Amen.

Chapter Seven

THE CHURCH, MARY, AND THE SAINTS

Thérèse was not a typical young nun. She was kind and devout and humble, of course, as were most of her fellow nuns. But Thérèse was also unconventional. She disliked retreats. She found prayer difficult. She had great trouble praying the rosary. She didn't care for spiritual reading, except for Scripture and a few other books. And in an age when frequent Communion was rare, she felt it should be encouraged.

Thérèse's love for the church, Mary, and the saints was marked by this strong thinking. Regarding frequent Communion, she didn't hesitate to point out that Jesus comes to earth every day not to lie in a golden ciborium but to rest in our hearts.

None of the sermons she heard about Mary impressed her in the least, especially those that presented Mary as a paragon of virtue, inaccessible to the ordinary person. She wished that she could have been a priest, she said, so that she could have preached about Mary as the holy but in many ways ordinary woman that she was.

As she lay dying, Thérèse kept near her bed various holy cards and pictures of the saints. She frequently appealed to the saints, and especially to the Blessed Virgin, in prayer. If they heard her, that was fine. If they didn't, she said, she loved them anyway. She never perceived them as exalted and unapproachable but as fellow travelers who had gone before her on the road of life.

In an age that tended to see religion as stern and unyielding, Thérèse spoke of God himself, his church, his mother, and the saints, with tremendous warmth and affection. The church was her home and these were her friends, her true family, those who accompanied her on the way home.

The Blessed in Heaven

I believe the blessed have great compassion on our miseries, they remember being weak and mortal like us, they committed the same faults, sustained the same combats, and their fraternal tenderness becomes greater than it was when they were on earth, and for this reason, they never cease protecting us and praying for us. (GC II 1173)

How different are the ways through which the Lord leads souls! In the lives of the saints, we find many of them who didn't want to leave anything of themselves behind after their death, not the smallest souvenir, not the least bit of writing.

On the contrary, there are others, like our holy mother St. Teresa [of Ávila], who have enriched the church with their lofty revelations, having no fears of revealing the secrets of the King in order that they may make him more loved and known by souls.

Which of these two types of saints is more pleasing to God? It seems to me . . . they are equally pleasing to him, since all of them followed the inspiration of the Holy Spirit. (SS Clarke 207)

Thérèse recounted the following incident in a conversation with her sister Pauline. The communion of saints was a source of great consolation to Thérèse.

Sister Marie of the Eucharist wanted to light the candles for a procession. She had no matches; however, seeing the little lamp which was burning in front of the relics, she approached it.

Alas, it was half out; there remained only a feeble glimmer on its blackened wick. She succeeded in lighting her candle from it, and with this candle, she lighted those of the whole community

It was, therefore, the half-extinguished little lamp which had produced all these beautiful flames which, in their turn, could produce an infinity of others and even light the whole universe. Nevertheless, it would always be the little lamp which would be first cause of all this light. How could the beautiful flames boast of having produced this fire, when they themselves were lighted with such a small spark?

It is the same with the communion of saints. Very often, without our knowing it, the graces and lights that we receive are due to a hidden soul, for God wills that the saints communicate grace to each other through prayer with great love, with a love much greater than that of a family, and even the most perfect family on earth.

How often have I thought that I may owe all the graces I've received to the prayers of a person who begged them from God for me, and whom I shall know only in heaven. . . .

In heaven, we shall not meet with indifferent glances, because all the elect will discover that they owe to each other the graces that merited the crown for them. (HLC 99–100)

Devotion to the Holy Eucharist

Thérèse described her first Communion as a total union with Jesus.

Ah, how sweet was that first kiss of Jesus! It was a kiss of love; I felt that I was loved, and I said: "I love you, and I give myself to you forever!" There were no demands made, no struggles, no sacrifices. . . . It was a fusion; there were no longer two, Thérèse had vanished as a drop of water is lost in the immensity of the ocean. Jesus alone remained. (SS Clarke 77)

The feeling of love Thérèse's experienced was so overwhelming that it moved her to tears. Those who were with her misunderstood the reason for her crying.

They did not understand that all the joy of heaven having entered my heart; this exiled heart was unable to bear it without shedding tears. (SS Clarke 77)

Thérèse longed to receive Communion every day, but that was not the custom of the time. On some occasions, for various reasons, however, she received more often than usual.

[Jesus] gave himself to me in holy Communion more frequently than I would have dared hope. I'd taken as a rule of conduct to receive, without missing a single one, the Communions my confessor permitted, allowing him to regulate the number and not asking. At this time in my life, I didn't have the boldness I now have, for I am very sure a soul must tell her confessor the attraction she feels to receive her God.

It is not to remain in a golden ciborium that he comes to us each day from heaven; it's to find another heaven, infinitely more dear to him than the first: the heaven of our soul, made to his image, the living temple of the adorable Trinity! (SS Clarke 104)

Thérèse's cousin, Marie Guérin, was excessively concerned over imagined sins. This scrupulosity prevented her from receiving Communion. She wrote to Thérèse, and Thérèse, only sixteen years old, responded with a letter that reveals a mature grasp of the power of the Eucharist. It was even more impressive since she wrote at a time when Communion was considered something of a rare privilege.

In 1910 this particular letter came to the attention of a priest working on Thérèse's cause for canonization. He brought it to Pope Pius X, who had written a decree urging Catholics to receive Communion more frequently. The pope called Thérèse's letter "most opportune" and told the priest that "we must hurry this cause" (GC I 569, n. 4).

Should I tell you something that has given me much sorrow? It is that my little Marie has given up her Communions. . . . Oh! What sorrow this has caused Jesus! . . .

The devil has to be very clever to mislead a soul in this way! But don't you know . . . that this is the only goal of his desires? The evil one knows well that he can't make a soul that wants to belong totally to Jesus to commit a sin, so he tries to make the soul believe it has.

It is already much for him to put disturbance in this soul, but to satisfy his rage something else is needed; he wants to deprive Jesus of a loved tabernacle, and, not being able to enter this sanctuary, he wants, at least, that it remain empty and without any master! . . .

When the devil has succeeded in drawing the soul away from holy Communion , he has won everything. . . . Don't listen to the devil, mock him, and go without any fear to receive Jesus in peace and love! . . .

[Thérèse], too, has passed through the martyrdom of scruples, but Jesus has given her the grace to receive Communion just the same. . . . I assure you that she knew this was the sole means of ridding herself of the devil, for when he sees that he is losing [wasting] his time, he leaves you in peace!

No, it is impossible that a heart "which rests only at the sight of the tabernacle" offend Jesus to the point of not being able to receive him; what offends him and what wounds his heart is the lack of confidence! . . .

Receive Communion often, very often. That is the only remedy if you want to be healed. (GC I 567–69)

Six weeks before her death, Thérèse had an insight into the importance of the Confiteor, the prayer of repentance said during the Mass.

How great the grace is that I received this morning when the priest began the Confiteor before giving me Communion. . . .

I saw Jesus very close to giving himself to me, and this confession appears to me as such a necessary humiliation. "I confess to Almighty God, to Blessed Virgin Mary, to all the saints, that I have sinned exceedingly."

Oh! Yes, I said to myself, they do well to beg pardon from God and all the saints for me at this moment. Like the publican, I felt I was a great sinner. I found God to be so merciful! I found it so touching to address oneself to the whole heavenly court to obtain God's pardon through its intercession.

Ah! I could hardly keep from crying, and when the sacred host touched my lips, I was really moved. How extraordinary it is to have experienced this at the Confiteor! (HLC 147)

The Holy Family

Thérèse saw the Holy Family as down-to-earth and ordinary, as she illustrates here. She speaks out against the many apocryphal stories that for centuries were popular among Christians.

How charming it will be in heaven to know everything that took place in the Holy Family! When little Jesus began to grow up, perhaps when he saw the Blessed Virgin fasting, he said to her: "I would really like to fast too." And the Blessed Virgin answered: "No, little Jesus, you are still too little, you haven't the strength." Or else perhaps she didn't dare hinder him from doing this.

And good St. Joseph! Oh! How I love him! He wasn't able to fast because of his work.

I can see him planing, then drying his forehead from time to time. Oh! How I pity him. It seems to me that their life was simple.

The country women came to speak familiarly with the Blessed Virgin. Sometimes they asked her to entrust her little Jesus to them so that he would go and play with their children. . . .

What does me a lot of good when I think of the Holy Family is to imagine a life that was very ordinary. It wasn't everything that they have told us or imagined. For example, that the child Jesus, after having formed some birds out of clay, breathed upon them and gave them life. Ah! No! Little Jesus didn't perform useless miracles like that, even to please his mother.

Why weren't they transported into Egypt by a miracle which would have been necessary and so easy for God. In the twinkling of an eye, they could have been brought there. No, everything in their life was done just as in our own.

How many troubles, disappointments! How many times did others make complaints to good St. Joseph! How many times did they refuse to pay him for his work!

Oh! How astonished we would be if we only knew how much they had to suffer! (HLC 159)

Mary and Her Maternal Love

Thérèse again takes up the theme of the ordinariness of Mary's life.

———◦———

How I would have loved to be a priest in order to preach about the Blessed Virgin! . . .

I'd first make people understand how little is known by us about her life. We shouldn't say unlikely things or things we don't know anything about! For example, that when she was very little, at the age of three, the Blessed Virgin went up to the temple to offer herself to God, burning with sentiments of love and extraordinary fervor. While perhaps she went there very simply out of obedience to her parents.

Again, why say with reference to the aged Simeon's prophetic words, that the Blessed Virgin had the passion of Jesus constantly before her mind from that moment onward? "And a sword shall pierce through your soul also" [Luke 2:35], the old man said. It wasn't for the present . . . it was a general prediction for the future.

For a sermon on the Blessed Virgin to please me and do me any good, I must see her real life, not her imagined life. I'm sure that her real life was very simple. They show her to us as unapproachable, but they should present her as imitable, bringing out her virtues, saying that she lived by faith, just like ourselves, giving proofs of this from the gospel, where we read: "And they did not understand the words which he spoke to them" [Luke 2:33]. (HLC 161)

Thérèse stresses Mary's maternal love, knowing that it is easier to approach her as mother than under her more exalted title as Queen of Heaven.

———————

We know very well that the Blessed Virgin is queen of heaven and earth, but she is more mother than queen; and we should not say, on account of her prerogatives, that she surpasses all the saints in glory just as the sun at its rising makes the stars disappear from sight. My God! How strange that would be! A mother who makes her children's glory vanish! I myself think just the contrary. I believe she'll increase the splendor of the elect very much.

Its good to speak about her prerogatives, but we should not stop at this, and if, in a sermon, we are obliged from beginning to end to exclaim and say: Ah! Ah! We would grow tired!

Who knows whether some soul would not reach the point of feeling a certain estrangement from a creature so superior and would not say: If things are such, it's better to go and shine as well as one is able in some little corner!

What the Blessed Virgin has more than we have is the privilege of not being able to sin, she was exempt from the stain of original sin; but on the other hand, she wasn't as fortunate as we are, since she didn't have a Blessed Virgin to love. And this is one more sweetness for us and one less sweetness for her! (HLC 161–62)

Thérèse insisted that Mary wanted not so much to be admired as to be imitated.

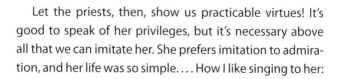

Let the priests, then, show us practicable virtues! It's good to speak of her privileges, but it's necessary above all that we can imitate her. She prefers imitation to admiration, and her life was so simple. . . . How I like singing to her:

The narrow road to heaven you have made visible . . . when practicing always the most humble virtues. (HLC 166)

Our Lady of Victories

When Thérèse was ten years old, she developed a mysterious illness that brought her close to death. Her symptoms included hallucinations and extreme fatigue. Thérèse said afterward that she felt the devil was at the root of the illness because he wanted to punish her for the harm her family would do him in the future.

When it seemed that there was no hope for Thérèse, her father wrote to the shrine of Our Lady of Victories in Paris and requested that a series of Masses be offered for Thérèse's recovery.

The Martins had a particular devotion to Our Lady of Victories and kept her statue in a place of honor. Mary had once spoken to Thérèse's mother as she prayed in front of it. That statue now stood beside Thérèse's bed. Her older sisters—Marie, Léonie, and Céline—were helping to care for her.

One Sunday (during the novena . . .), Marie went out into the garden, leaving me with Léonie, who was reading near the window.

After a few minutes I started calling almost silently, "Mama . . . Mama," . . . and finally Marie came back in. I saw her clearly when she entered, but I couldn't say that I recognized her, and I continued to call out ever louder, "Mama." . . .

[Marie] got down on her knees beside my bed with Léonie and Céline, and then, turning toward the Blessed Virgin, and praying with the fervor of a mother who asking for the life of her child, Marie obtained what she desired.

Finding no help on earth, poor little Thérèse has turned toward her heavenly mother. She was praying to her with all her heart to finally have pity on her.

Suddenly the Blessed Virgin seemed beautiful to me, so beautiful that I had never seen anything so beautiful. Her face was breathing inexpressible goodness and tenderness, but what penetrated right to the depths of my soul was the "lovely smile of the Blessed Virgin." Then all my sufferings melted away, and two big tears burst from my eyelids and streaked silently down my cheeks—but these were tears of an unadulterated joy. Oh! I thought, the Blessed Virgin smiled at me, how happy I am. . . .

I . . . saw Marie, who was watching me with love. She seemed moved, and seemed to suspect the favor that the Blessed Virgin had granted me. Oh! It was to her, to her touching prayers, that I owed the grace of the smile of the Queen of Heaven. When she saw my gaze fixed on the

Blessed Virgin, she had said to herself, "Thérèse has been healed!" Yes, the little flower was going to be born anew to life. (SS Edmonson 64–66)

After Thérèse's miraculous healing, Marie goaded her into describing exactly what she had seen when Mary smiled. Thérèse had wanted to keep this secret, fearing that talking about it would diminish the incident.

In fact, Thérèse later recalled, the moment she told Marie what she had seen, her happiness disappeared, causing her to regret speaking. Because of this, the memory of the grace she received tormented her for four years.

She only found peace, she said, on the pilgrimage the Martins took to Paris and Italy. While in Paris, Thérèse's father brought her to the Church of Our Lady of Victories, and there Thérèse received confirmation that Mary had indeed brought about her healing from the mysterious illness.

We reached Paris in the morning and commenced our visit without any delay. Poor little father tired himself trying to please us, and very soon we saw all the marvels of the capital. I myself found only one which filled me with delight, Our Lady of Victories!

Ah! What I felt kneeling at her feet cannot be expressed. The graces she granted me so moved me that my happiness found expression only in tears, just as on the day of my first Communion. The Blessed Virgin made me feel it was really herself who smiled on me and brought about my cure.

I understood she was watching over me, that I was her child. I could no longer give her any other name but "Mamma," as this appeared ever so much more tender than "Mother."

How fervently I begged her to protect me always, to bring to fruition as quickly as possible my dream of hiding beneath the shadow of her virginal mantle! This was one of my first desires as a child. When growing up, I understood it was at Carmel I would truly find the Blessed Virgin's mantle, and towards this fertile mount I directed all my desires. (SS Clarke 123)

The statue of Our Lady of Victories stood by Thérèse's bed during her childhood illness. Years later, it was placed by her bed as she lay dying in the infirmary.

The convent began a novena to Our Lady of Victories when it became apparent that Thérèse was seriously ill. The sisters were disappointed, but Thérèse herself never seemed to expect another miracle. She found great consolation, however, in gazing at the statue and in praying to Mary.

I'm perhaps losing my wits. Oh! If only they knew the weakness I'm experiencing. Last night, I couldn't take any more: I begged the Blessed Virgin to hold my head in her hands so that I could take my sufferings. (HLC 154)

O my God! . . . I love God! . . . O good Blessed Virgin, come to my aid! . . . If this is the agony, what is death?! (HLC 204)

When her sufferings reached a pitch, her mother prioress assured her that soon she'd be with "the Blessed Virgin and the child Jesus."

O Mother, present me quickly to the Blessed Virgin. I'm a baby who can't stand any more. Prepare me for death! (HLC 205)

Reflection

Like all the great saints, Thérèse belonged whole-heartedly to the church. She wasn't blind to its problems, and she had firsthand experience of the shortcomings of its leaders. She had no false hopes, no illusions, and no dangerous sentimentalism.

Thérèse was able to accept the good with the bad because she knew that this was where she would best meet Jesus. Everything she needed for the journey—God himself, the Eucharist, the angels, Mary, the saints, the sacraments—she found in the church.

Prayer

Lord, thank you for your mother. Help me to love her and trust her as you did when you were on earth. Thank you for the saints. They were sinners, as we are sinners. They understand our weaknesses and are ready to intercede for us. Help me to draw close to them, to meet them as friends who will help me grow closer to you. Through Christ our Lord, Amen.

Chapter Eight

GIVING SPIRITUAL DIRECTION: REFLECTING TRUTH

Although Thérèse never bore the official title of novice mistress, she had the responsibility of training the young Carmelites—some of whom were older than she was—from the spring of 1893, when she herself was only twenty, until her strength gave out in 1897.

If the novices expected to glide easily through their formation under the gentle, humble Thérèse, they had a rude awakening. She was tough and unrelenting in her determination to shape them.

She was a soldier and not afraid of combat, she said in reference to her struggles with one difficult novice. On her deathbed, Thérèse had to correct that same novice. "Didn't I tell you," she said, "that I would die with my weapons in my hand?" (HLC 236)

Some of what Thérèse has to say about spiritual direction does not apply to laypeople. She was training women for the religious life and worked within the structure of their vows. When she spoke of obedience, for example, she was often talking about the very strict obedience to authority demanded by the Carmelite vow.

On the other hand, much of what Thérèse offers is useful for anyone concerned with the spiritual development of others. Even parents can adapt and apply some of Thérèse's advice to the formation of their children.

Thérèse excelled at her task, and in spite of her occasional severity, the novices loved her. Mother de Gonzague said that Thérèse fulfilled these duties with the novices with a perfection and wisdom matched only by her love for God.

She was able to do so with serenity because of her unwavering faith in the Lord. Thérèse didn't manipulate, plead, bargain, or berate. She simply did her best and then entrusted the particular novice or situation to the Lord.

"To the right and to the left, I throw to my little birds the good grain that God places in my hands. And then I let things take their course! I busy myself with it no more. . . . God tells me: 'Give, give always, without being concerned about the results'" (HLC 44).

Guiding Souls

Thérèse gave God the credit for her successes as director of the novices.

I saw immediately that the task was beyond my strength. . . . I felt that the only thing necessary was to unite myself more and more to Jesus and that "all these things will be given to you besides" [Matthew 6:33]. In fact, never was my hope mistaken, for God saw fit to fill my little hand as many times as it was necessary for nourishing the soul of my sisters.

I admit . . . that if I had depended in the least on my own strength, I would very soon have had to give up. From a distance it appears all roses to do good to souls, making them love God more and molding them according to one's personal views and ideas.

At close range it is totally the contrary, the roses disappear; one feels that to do good is as impossible without God's help as to make the sun shine at night.

One feels it is absolutely necessary to forget one's likings, one's personal conceptions, and to guide souls along the road which Jesus has traced out for them without trying to make them walk one's own way. (SS Clarke 238)

I placed myself in God's arms, like a little child, and, hiding my face in his hair, I told him, "Lord, I'm too little to feed your children. If you want to give them through me what is proper for each one, fill my little hand, and without leaving your arms, without turning my head, I'll give your treasures to the soul who comes to me to ask for her food.

"If she finds it according to her taste, I'll know that it's not to me but to you that she owes it. On the other hand, if she complains about what I present to her and finds it bitter, my peace won't be troubled. I'll try to persuade her that this food comes from you, and I'll take care not to look for any other food for her." (SS Edmonson 268)

By teaching others, I'd learned a great deal. I saw first of all that all souls have just about the same struggles, but they're so different from another point of view that I have no trouble understanding what Fr. Pichon [Thérèse's confessor] said: "There's a much greater difference among souls than there is among faces." Therefore it's impossible to act with all of them in the same way.

With certain souls, I feel that I have to make myself little, not being afraid to humble myself by admitting my struggles, my defeats. Seeing that I have the same weakness as they do, my dear sisters in turn confess to me the faults that they reproach themselves for, and they rejoice that I understand them through experience.

With others I've seen that on the contrary, in order to do them good I have to have a great deal of firmness and never take back anything once I've said it. In that case, taking a low place wouldn't be humility, but weakness. (SS Edmonson 270–71)

Nothing but the truth—that's what Thérèse gave her novices. If they didn't want to hear it, she said, they ought to avoid her.

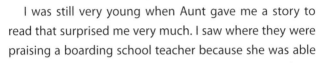

I was still very young when Aunt gave me a story to read that surprised me very much. I saw where they were praising a boarding school teacher because she was able to extricate herself cleverly from certain situations without offending anyone.

I took note above all of this statement: "She said to this one: You're not wrong; to that one, You are right." And I thought to myself: This is not good! This teacher should have had no fear and should have told her little girls that they were wrong when this was the truth.

And even now I haven't changed my opinion. I've had a lot of trouble over it, I admit, for it's always so easy to place the blame on the absent, and this immediately calms the one who is complaining.

Yes, but it is just the contrary with me. If I'm not loved, that's just too bad! I tell the whole truth, and if anyone doesn't wish to know the truth, let her not come looking for me. (HLC 38)

Before I left the world, God gave me the consolation of contemplating at close range the souls of little children. . . .

A poor woman, a relative of our maid, died when still very young and left three very little children; during the woman's illness, we took care of the two little girls; the older one was not yet six. I spent the whole day with them, and it was a great pleasure for me to see with what simplicity they believed everything I said....

I spoke to them about the eternal rewards that little Jesus would give in heaven to good little children. The older one, whose reason was beginning to develop, looked at me with eyes that were bright with joy, asking me a thousand charming questions about little Jesus and his beautiful heaven....

Seeing innocent souls at such close range, I understood what a misfortune it was when they were not formed in their early years, when they are soft as wax upon which one can imprint either virtue or vice. I understood, too, what Jesus said: "But whoever causes one of these little ones to sin, it were better for him to have a great millstone fastened round his neck and to be drowned in the depths of the sea!" [Matthew 18:6]. Ah! How many souls would have reached sanctity had they been well directed! (SS Clarke 112–13)

Relying on God and Letting Go of Self-Interest

In a conversation with Pauline, Thérèse gives us a glimpse of how she relied on God to help her direct the novices. Sister Geneviève was her older sister Céline, who, like all the novices, spent time privately with Thérèse.

When Sister Geneviève used to come to visit me, I wasn't able to say all I wanted to say in a half hour. Then, during the week, whenever I had a thought or else was sorry for having forgotten to tell her something, I would ask God to let her know and understand what I was thinking about and in the next visit she'd speak to me exactly about the thing I had asked God to let her know.

At the beginning, when she was really suffering and I was unable to console her, I would leave the visit with a heavy heart, but I soon understood it wasn't I who could console anyone; and then I was no longer troubled when she left very sad.

I begged God to supply for my weakness, and I felt he answered me. I would see this in the following visit. Since that time, whenever I involuntarily caused anyone any trouble, I would beg God to repair it, and then I no longer tormented myself with the matter. (HLC 93)

Thérèse approached the spiritual direction of others with a complete lack of self-interest. She didn't care what the novices thought of her, and she wasn't even concerned that her work bear fruit. She did her

Spiritual Treasures from St. Thérèse of Lisieux

best and then left the situation in God's hands. This not only freed her from anxiety but forced each novice to take responsibility for her own development.

———

Ever since I took over the novitiate, my life has been one of war and struggle. But the good God has done the work for me. I have labored for him and my soul has made astounding progress.

My only desire has been to please him; consequently I have not worried over what others might be thinking or saying about me. I have not sought to be loved for myself, nor have I desired that my efforts bear fruit. True, we must sow the seed of goodness on all sides, but if it does not spring up, what matter! Our lot is to work, the victory is for Jesus.

When there is question of doing good to our neighbor, we must let nothing deter us nor pass over anything to make things easier for ourselves. As for reprimands, our intention in giving them must be directed first to the glory of God and must not spring from a desire to succeed in enlightening the novices. (MSST 5–6)

No Guilt about Reprimands

Therese's advice on correction can be applied in many situations. Kindness is a virtue, but those in authority need to offer correction with courage, not falling prey to guilt or sentimentalism.

We should never allow kindness to degenerate into weakness. When we have scolded someone with just reason, we must leave the matter there, without allowing ourselves to be touched to the point of tormenting ourselves for having caused pain or at seeing someone suffer and cry. To run after the afflicted one to console her does more harm than good. Leaving her to herself forces her to have recourse to God. . . .

Otherwise, accustomed to receiving consolation after a merited reprimand, she will always act, in the same circumstances, like a spoiled child. (HLC 38)

Reflection

Giving and receiving direction is a touchy business. Both parties may fall victim to pride, one convinced that the advice is helpful, the other convinced that the director is not sensitive to his or her needs. In fact, both may be completely wrong.

Terrible damage has been done not only through misguided spiritual direction but also through the stubborn refusal to accept good advice. Thérèse skirted these hazards by leaving each situation to the

Lord and not insisting on her own way. She stayed close to God, gave the direction she thought best, and left the consequences to the Lord.

Prayer

Lord, help me to welcome into my life all those people whose advice and insight can lead me closer to you. Sometimes what they have to say may be painful, and I won't want to hear it. Help me to overcome my resistance so that I can be all that you've called me to be. Through Christ our Lord, Amen.

Chapter Nine

Zeal, Intercessory Prayer, and Conversion

No saint seems a less likely candidate for patron saint of the missions than Thérèse of Lisieux. Yet she shares that honor with St. Francis Xavier, a widely traveled and more logical choice. Francis, it is said, converted hundreds of thousands and endured harrowing conditions during his travels through the east.

Thérèse, on the other hand, never left her cloister for the nine years of her religious life, apparently converted no one, wrote no treatises on evangelization, never preached to large crowds, never baptized anyone, and never engaged in fund raising. To all appearances, she did nothing more than pursue her Little Way among the twenty-five or so nuns of her own convent.

But the church recognizes in Thérèse a most unusual and intense missionary spirit: she proposes to "spend her heaven doing good on earth," bringing souls to Jesus. "If God answers my desires," she said, "my heaven will be spent on earth until the end of the world" (HLC 102).

Not even Francis, the consummate missionary, makes such an extravagant claim. Earthbound, he accomplished miraculous conversions. Thérèse couldn't compete with him in life, but she has matched him in death. Shortly after she died, accounts of restored relationships, conversions, and healings granted through her intercession began to pour into the Carmel of Lisieux.

The foundation for Thérèse's heavenly activity, however, was the zeal for souls that gripped her on earth. She was consumed with a thirst for souls, she said. Her life was nothing less than an apostolate of prayer and suffering for sinners. Even on her deathbed, in the midst of terrible pain, she insisted that the prayers offered for her relief be offered, instead, on behalf of sinners.

Thérèse's zeal sprang from her love for God and his love for her. This was too good to keep to herself. The point of her life, she said, was to love Jesus wholeheartedly and to bring others to love him with that same consuming passion.

A Fisher of Souls

Even before Thérèse entered the convent, she was convinced that Jesus had made her "a fisher of souls." She said that she experienced a tremendous desire to work for the conversion of sinners. She had her first success in this line when she prayed for the salvation of an unrepentant murderer named Pranzini. The event was crucial in launching Thérèse on her apostolate of prayer. Céline offered to join her in interceding for the man.

———

I would have wished all creatures would unite with me to beg grace for the guilty man [Pranzini]. I felt in the depths of my heart certain that our desires would be granted, but to obtain courage to pray for sinners I told God I was sure he would pardon the poor, unfortunate Pranzini. . . . I was absolutely confident in the mercy of Jesus. But I was begging him for a "sign" of repentance only for my own simple consolation.

My prayer was answered to the letter! In spite of Papa's prohibition that we read no papers, I didn't think I was disobeying when reading the passages pertaining to Pranzini. The day after his execution I found the newspaper *La Croix*. I opened it quickly and what did I see? Ah! My tears betrayed my emotion and I was obliged to hide.

Pranzini had not gone to confession. He had mounted the scaffold and was preparing to place his head in the formidable opening [of the guillotine], when suddenly, seized by an inspiration, he turned, took hold of the crucifix the priest was holding out to him and kissed the sacred wounds three times! Then his soul went to receive the merciful sentence of him who declares that in heaven there will be more joy over one sinner who does penance than over ninety-nine just who have no need of repentance [Luke 15:7]!

I had obtained the "sign" I requested, and this sign was a perfect replica of the grace Jesus had given me when he attracted me to pray for sinners. . . .

After this unique grace my desire to save souls grew each day, and I seemed to hear Jesus say to me what he had said to the Samaritan woman: "Give me to drink!" [John 4:7]. It was a true interchange of love: to souls I was giving the blood of Jesus, to Jesus I was offering these same souls refreshed by the divine dew. I slaked his thirst and the more I gave him to drink, the more the thirst of my poor little soul [for the conversion of sinners] increased. (SS Clarke 100)

One Sunday, looking at a picture of our Lord on the cross, I was struck by the blood flowing from one of the divine hands. I felt a great pang of sorrow when thinking this blood was falling to the ground without anyone's hastening to gather it up.

I was resolved to remain in spirit at the foot of the cross and to receive the divine dew. I understood I was then to pour it out upon souls.

The cry of Jesus on the cross sounded continually in my heart: "I thirst!" These words ignited within me an unknown and very living fire. I wanted to give my beloved to drink, and I felt myself consumed with a thirst for souls. . . . I burned with the desire to snatch [great sinners] from the eternal flames. (SS Clarke 99)

Thérèse was asked to correspond with a missionary priest who requested the prayers and support of one of the nuns of Carmel. She wrote to him concerning her zeal for souls.

———————⚬———————

I do not want you to ask God to deliver me from the flames of purgatory; Saint Teresa [of Ávila] said to her daughters when they wanted to pray for her: "What does it matter to me to remain until the end of the world in purgatory if through my prayers I save a single soul."

These words find an echo in my heart. I would like to save souls and forget myself for them; I would like to save them even after my death. So I would be happy if you were to say . . . "My God, allow my sister to make you still loved." (GC II 1072)

When I was beginning to learn the history of France, the account of Joan of Arc's exploits delighted me; I felt in my heart the desire and the courage to imitate her. It seemed the Lord destined me, too, for great things.

I was not mistaken, but instead of voices from heaven inviting me to combat, I heard in the depths of my soul a gentler and stronger voice, that of the Spouse of Virgins, who was calling me to other exploits, to more glorious conquests, and into Carmel's solitude.

I understood my mission was not to have a mortal king crowned but to make the King of Heaven loved, to submit to him the kingdom of hearts. (GC II 1085)

One day when I was thinking of what I could do to save souls, a word of the gospel gave me a real light. In days gone by, Jesus said to his disciples when showing them the fields of ripe corn: "Lift up your eyes and see how the fields are already white enough to be harvested," and a little later: "In truth, the harvest is abundant but the number of laborers is small. Ask then the master of the harvest to send laborers."

What a mystery! Is not Jesus all-powerful? Are not creatures his who made them? Why, then, does Jesus say: "Ask the Lord of the harvest that he send some workers"? Why?

Ah! It is because Jesus has so incomprehensible a love for us that he wills that we have a share with him in the salvation of souls. He wills to do nothing without us. The creator of the universe awaits the prayer of a poor little soul to save other souls redeemed like it at the price of all his blood. (GC II 753)

I hold nothing in my hands. Everything I have, everything I merit, is for the church and for souls. (HLC 91)

Let us not grow tired of prayer; confidence works miracles. And Jesus said to Blessed Mary Margaret: "one just soul has so much power over my heart that it can obtain pardon for a thousand criminals." (GC II 729)

Praying for Priests

At the direction of St. Teresa of Ávila, the sixteenth-century reformer of the Carmelite order, the Carmelites have made a specific commitment to pray for priests.

When Thérèse entered the order, she said that she had come "to save souls and especially to pray for priests." The next few selections indicate how seriously she took that commitment.

Let us pray for priests; each day shows how few the friends of Jesus are. It seems to me this is what he must feel the most, ingratitude, especially when seeing souls

181

who are consecrated to him giving to others a heart that belongs to him in so absolute a way. (GC II 708)

On her trip to Rome, Thérèse gained insight into the importance of praying for priests.

Having never lived close [to priests], I was not able to understand the principle aim of . . . Carmel. To pray for sinners attracted me, but to pray for the souls of priests whom I believed to be as pure as crystal seemed puzzling to me!

I understood my vocation in Italy and that's not going too far in search of such useful knowledge. I lived in the company of many saintly priests for a month, and I learned that, though their dignity raises them above the angels, they are nevertheless weak and fragile men.

If holy priests, whom Jesus in his gospel calls "the salt of the earth," show in their conduct their extreme need for prayers, what is to be said of those who are tepid? Didn't Jesus say too: "If the salt loses its flavor, wherewith will it be salted?" [Matthew 5:13].

How beautiful is the vocation . . . which has as its aim the preservation of the salt destined for souls! This is Carmel's vocation since the sole purpose of our prayers and sacrifices is to be the apostle of the apostles. We are to pray for them while they are preaching to souls through their words and especially their example. (SS Clarke 122)

In two letters to Céline, Thérèse conveys a sense of urgency in the matter of praying for priests.

Céline, during the short moments that remain to us, let us not lose our time. Let us save souls. Souls are being lost like flakes of snow, and Jesus weeps. . . .

Let us live for souls, let us be apostles, let us save especially the souls of priests; these souls should be more transparent than crystal.

Alas, how many bad priests [there are], priests who are not holy enough. Let us pray, let us suffer for them, and, on the last day, Jesus will be grateful. We shall give him souls! (GC I 578)

Céline, I feel that Jesus is asking both of us to quench his thirst by giving him souls, the souls of priests especially. . . . We are so insignificant and yet Jesus wills that the salvation of souls depends on the sacrifices of our love. He is begging souls from us. (GC I 587–88)

Spending Heaven Doing Good on Earth

Thérèse wanted so much to win souls for Jesus that she was determined to continue her work for the church even after her death.

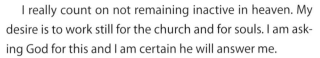

I really count on not remaining inactive in heaven. My desire is to work still for the church and for souls. I am asking God for this and I am certain he will answer me.

Are not the angels continually occupied with us without their ever ceasing to see the divine face and to lose themselves in the ocean of love without shores? Why would Jesus not allow me to imitate them? (GC II 1142)

I feel . . . my mission is about to begin, my mission of making God loved as I love him, of giving my little way to souls. If God answers my desires, my heaven will be spent on earth until the end of the world.

Yes, I want to spend my heaven in doing good on earth. That isn't impossible, since from the bosom of the beatific vision, the angels watch over us.

I can't make heaven a feast of rejoicing; I can't rest as long as there are souls to be saved. But when the angel will have said: "Time is no more!" [Revelation 10:6] then I will take my rest; I'll be able to rejoice, because the number of the elect will be complete and because all will have entered into joy and repose. (HLC 102)

I am not looking forward to enjoyment and rest in heaven; all that attracts me is love: to love, to be loved, and to return to the world to make God loved, to help missionaries, priests and the whole church. I want to spend my heaven doing good on earth. (STL 68)

Reflection

There was no conflict in Thérèse's mind between her intense desire to save souls and the cloistered life. She knew she didn't need to be on the spot in order to bring an individual to the Lord.

All Thérèse's missionary work, all her "evangelization," took place through prayer and sacrifice. "Prayer is my greatest weapon," she once said, and she wielded it effectively.

Thérèse gets us back to the basics of evangelization: not techniques, books, or programs but prayer, sacrifice, and a heart set on God.

Prayer

Lord, give me a zealous heart. Renew in me the desire to bring others to you. When I do bring your word to those who don't know you, keep me humble and close to you. May your own compassion fill and guide me. Through Christ our Lord, Amen.

Appendix

TIME LINE OF THÉRÈSE'S LIFE

Jan. 2, 1873	Thérèse is born in Alençon, France.
Aug. 28, 1877	Zélie Martin (Thérèse's mother) dies.
Aug. 29, 1877	Thérèse asks Pauline to be her mother.
Nov. 1877	The Martins move to Lisieux to be near their cousins.
Oct. 2, 1882	Pauline enters the Carmel at Lisieux.
Oct. 3, 1882	Thérèse begins school at the Benedictine Abbey in Lisieux.
Mar.–May 1883	Thérèse is seriously ill.
May 13, 1883	Thérèse is cured after seeing a statue of the Blessed Virgin smile.
May 8, 1884	Thérèse receives her first Communion.
May 22, 1884	Thérèse receives the willingness to suffer.
June 14, 1884	Thérèse receives the Sacrament of Confirmation and, with it, the strength to suffer.
Oct. 15, 1886	Marie enters the Carmel at Lisieux.
Dec. 25, 1886	Thérèse's "Christmas conversion." She is freed from hypersensitivity and receives the desire to save souls.
May 1, 1887	Louis Martin suffers a small stroke.

May 29, 1887	Louis gives Thérèse permission to enter the Carmelite Order.
July 13, 1887	Thérèse begins to pray for the conversion of the murderer Pranzini.
Sept. 1, 1887	Thérèse learns of Pranzini's conversion before his execution.
Nov. 20, 1887	Thérèse appeals to the pope to allow her to enter Carmel.
Apr. 9, 1888	Thérèse enters the Carmel at Lisieux.
June 1888	Further decline of Louis Martin; he flees to Le Havre.
Jan. 10, 1889	Thérèse receives the habit.
Feb. 12, 1889	Louis Martin in Bon Sauveur Hospital.
Jan. 8, 1890	Thérèse makes her profession.
Sept. 24, 1890	Thérèse receives the veil.
May 12, 1892	Louis Martin makes a final visit to the Lisieux Carmel.
Feb. 20, 1893	Pauline is elected prioress; asks Thérèse to help in the formation of novices.
July 29, 1894	Louis Martin dies.
Sept. 14, 1894	Céline enters the Carmel at Lisieux.
Dec. 1894	Pauline asks Thérèse to write down memories of her childhood.
June 11, 1895	Thérèse offers herself as a victim of merciful love; Céline joins her in this offering.

Aug. 15, 1895	Marie Guérin, the Martins' cousin, enters the Carmel at Lisieux.
Mar. 21, 1896	Marie de Gonzague is elected prioress again.
Apr. 2–3, 1896	Thérèse coughs up blood.
Apr. 5, 1896	Thérèse begins her trial of faith.
Sept. 13, 1896	Thérèse begins to write reflections on love and her Little Way for her sister Marie. They will be added to Thérèse's autobiography.
Apr. 1897	Thérèse becomes seriously ill.
June 3, 1897	Thérèse continues her autobiography at the request of Mother Marie.
Aug. 19, 1897	Thérèse receives Communion for the last time.
Sept. 30, 1897	Thérèse dies at about 7:20 p.m.
Sept. 30, 1898	Two thousand copies of *Story of a Soul* arc printed.
Jun. 10, 1914	Pope Pius X signs the decree for the introduction of Thérèse's cause for canonization.
Apr. 29, 1923	Thérèse is beatified.
May 17, 1925	Thérèse is canonized. October 1 becomes the feast day of St. Thérèse.
Oct. 19, 1997	Pope John Paul II proclaims Thérèse a doctor of the church.

Acknowledgments

From *Story of a Soul,* translated by John Clarke, OCD. Copyright © 1975, 1976, 1996 by Washington Province of Discalced Carmelites, ICS Publications, 2131 Lincoln Road, NE, Washington, DC 20002-1199 USA. www.icspublications.org.

From *General Correspondence Volume One,* translated by John Clarke, OCD. Copyright © 1982 by Washington Province of Discalced Carmelites, ICS Publications, 2131 Lincoln Road, NE, Washington, DC 20002-1199 USA. www.icspublications.org.

From *General Correspondence Volume Two,* translated by John Clarke, OCD. Copyright © 1988 by Washington Province of Discalced Carmelites, ICS Publications, 2131 Lincoln Road, NE, Washington, DC 20002-1199 USA. www.icspublications.org.

From *St. Thérèse of Lisieux: Her Last Conversations,* translated by John Clarke, OCD. Copyright © 1977 by Washington Province of Discalced Carmelites, ICS Publications, 2131 Lincoln Road, NE, Washington, DC 20002-1199 USA. www.icspublications.org.

The Story of a Soul: St. Thérèse of Lisieux, translated and edited by Robert J. Edmonson, CJ. Copyright © 2006 by Paraclete Press Inc. Used by permission of Paraclete Press. www.paracletepress.com.

Sr. Geneviève of the Holy Face, *My Sister Saint Thérèse,* translated by the Carmelite Sisters of New York Conseils et Souvenirs. Copyright © 1997, Tan Books, Rockford, IL.

Also from The Word Among Us Press

Everything Is Grace
The Life and Way of Thérèse of Lisieux

Thérèse of Lisieux has been called the greatest saint of modern times, but some view her spirituality as overly sentimental. Thérèse's "little way" is really the gospel message—a message that can best be understood in the context of her life. Includes photographs of Thérèse as a young girl and throughout her life.
352 pages, 6 x 9, softcover,
Item# BSTLE7

Praying with Thérèse of Lisieux

Thérèse knew that God led her, with all her inadequacies, to holiness. She assures us that God can do the same for us.
160 pages, 5¼ x 8, softcover,
Item# BSMUE3